POOLING MONEY

YASUYUKI FUCHITA
ROBERT E. LITAN
Editors

POOLING MONEY

The Future of Mutual Funds

NOMURA INSTITUTE OF CAPITAL MARKETS RESEARCH
Tokyo

BROOKINGS INSTITUTION PRESS
Washington, D.C.

HG
4930
.P57
2008

Copyright © 2008
THE BROOKINGS INSTITUTION
NOMURA INSTITUTE OF CAPITAL MARKETS RESEARCH

All rights reserved. No part of this publication may be reproduced or
transmitted in any form or by any means without permission in writing from
the Brookings Institution Press.

ᴄᴏᴜ

Pooling Money: The Future of Mutual Funds may be ordered from:
BROOKINGS INSTITUTION PRESS, c/o HFS
P.O. Box 50370, Baltimore, MD 21211-4370
Tel.: 800/537-5487; 410/516-6956; Fax: 410/516-6998
Internet: www.brookings.edu

Library of Congress Cataloging-in-Publication data
Pooling money : the future of mutual funds / Yasuyuki Fuchita, Robert E. Litan, editors.
    p.   cm.
    Papers presented at a conference held organized by the Brookings Institution and the
Nomura Institute of Capital Markets Research, held at the Brookings Institution on
Oct. 18, 2007.
    Summary: "Experts from the United States and Japan look at forces of change in their
securities markets and offer their views of the future for mutual funds and other forms of
securities diversification"-Provided by publisher.
    Includes bibliographical references and index.
    ISBN 978-0-8157-2985-3 (pbk. : alk. paper)
    1. Mutual funds-United States-Congresses.   2. Mutual funds-Japan-Congresses.   3.
Mutual funds-Europe-Congresses.   I. Fuchita, Yasuyuki, 1958–   II. Litan, Robert E.,
1950–   III. Brookings Institution.   IV. Nomura Institute of Capital Markets Research.

HG4930.P57 2008
332.63'27-dc22   2008018755

9 8 7 6 5 4 3 2 1

The paper used in this publication meets minimum requirements of the
American National Standard for Information Sciences—Permanence of Paper for
Printed Library Materials: ANSI Z39.48-1992.

Typeset in Adobe Garamond

Composition by R. Lynn Rivenbark
Macon, Georgia

Printed by R. R. Donnelley
Harrisonburg, Virginia

Contents

University Libraries
Carnegie Mellon University
Pittsburgh, PA 15213-3890

v

Preface

THE BROOKINGS INSTITUTION and the Nomura Institute of Capital Markets Research have joined in a collaborative project, headed by Robert Litan, a Brookings senior fellow, and Yasuyuki Fuchita, director of the Nomura Institute of Capital Markets Research, to conduct research in selected topics of financial market structure and regulation.

This project convenes an annual conference on a defined topic in the fall of each year at Brookings, bringing together authors of papers and other experts to discuss and comment on them. The papers are then revised and published by the Brookings Institution and the Tokyo Club Foundation for Global Studies. This is the third conference volume, following *Financial Gatekeepers: Can They Protect Investors?* (2006) and *New Financial Instruments and Institutions: Opportunities and Policy Challenges* (2007).

The current volume is the result of a meeting on October 18, 2007, that focused on mutual funds in the United States, Europe, and Japan and possible future scenarios for mutual funds and their sponsors in those markets. All of the papers and comments represent the views of the authors and not necessarily those of the staff, officers, or trustees of the Brookings Institution or the Nomura Institute.

David Burke provided research assistance; Eric Haven checked for factual accuracy of the manuscript; and Teresa Wheatley and Lindsey Wilson organized the conference and provided administrative assistance.

YASUYUKI FUCHITA
ROBERT E. LITAN

Introduction
Mutual Funds:
Looking Back and Ahead

ONE OF THE cardinal rules of investing is not to put all of one's investment "eggs" in one basket. Investors can lower the risk that they run to achieve a given rate of return—or achieve higher returns for a given level of risk—by diversifying across and within broad categories, most commonly equities and bonds.

The mutual fund industry, dating from the formation of investment trusts more than two centuries ago, owes its origin to this simple insight: by pooling funds from a large number of investors and placing the funds into portfolios of financial instruments, mutual funds provide a more efficient means of diversification than individuals can achieve by investing on their own in specific stocks and bonds.

Mutual funds are of two basic types, closed- and open-end funds. Closed-end funds hold a fixed number of securities, with a fixed number of outstanding shares, which are traded in the open market as individual equities. The price of the shares thus is set in the market and often falls short of the fund's liquidation value per share. Open-end funds, in contrast, are continuously accepting (and in some cases redeeming) shares and investing the proceeds in a changing portfolio of securities. The shares are bought and sold at the fund's "net asset value," or the per share market value of all of the securities held by the fund, typically calculated from prices on the preceding trading day. Open-end funds have proven to be far more popular than closed-end funds, and unless otherwise noted, the discussion

I

of mutual funds or the mutual fund industry in this book refers specifically to open-end funds.

The mutual fund industry has enjoyed especially rapid growth since the end of World War II, a product of growth in income and wealth in developed economies (which fueled rising fund inflows) and the rise in stock prices (which increased the value of the monies invested). In the United States, for example, mutual funds held roughly $10 trillion in assets at year-end 2006, up from just $50 billion in the late 1960s. Worldwide, mutual fund assets exceeded $21 trillion at year-end 2006, a total that also had multiplied many times over the same period.

Mutual funds have grown not only in asset size but also in number. Currently more than 8,000 individual mutual funds are offered in the United States by roughly 500 mutual fund sponsors. Many more thousands of funds or their equivalents are in operation elsewhere throughout the world.

The large number of funds reflects the presence of many different types of funds, some that invest in both stocks and bonds of various types and many others that specialize in certain types of securities: large- and small-cap stocks, funds for virtually every industry sector, funds that mimic certain well-known stock indexes (the S&P 500 and the Dow-Jones averages or broader indexes, such as the Russell 3000), country funds, funds for different regions of the world, and funds that invest in various types of bonds of varying maturities.

Yet even as mutual fund assets have grown and choices among them have multiplied, it is not clear—as it once may have been—where this particular asset vehicle and the industry that has generated it are headed. New methods and options for efficient diversification have arisen—exchange-traded funds, or ETFs (instruments that trade like stocks and whose value is tied to some index); separately managed accounts offered by brokerage competitors; and limited partnerships in hedge funds and private equity funds (for wealthy investors)—and they are rapidly gaining ground on mutual funds. Meanwhile, the regulation of mutual funds themselves has been in flux, at least in some quarters. The scandals earlier in this decade in the United States over the "late trading" of fund shares by certain clients, coupled with criticism of fund fees, have sparked interest in strengthening oversight of funds. Meanwhile, the growing use of the Internet by investors to access information and to buy and sell individual securities as well as mutual funds and competing diversification vehicles is likely to lead eventually to major changes in the way that funds are required to disclose their investment objectives and performance and in the way that shareholders vote their shares.

Given the importance of mutual funds and the policy issues related to them, the Brookings Institution and the Tokyo Club convened their fourth annual joint conference on financial markets on October 18, 2007, at the Brookings Institution to examine the future of mutual funds as investment instruments and the future of the industry itself. This book presents the papers written for the conference and formal comments on the papers. We summarize here some of the key arguments and conclusions found in the presentations.

Mutual Funds in the United States

Because the fund industry and investor base are most developed in the United States, it is appropriate to begin with an analysis of the U.S. market. Paula Tkac of the Federal Reserve Bank of Atlanta takes up the challenge in chapter 1, first by describing the developments that have been most pronounced in the industry in the recent past and then by projecting the key trends that she expects to dominate fund activity in the foreseeable future.

Looking back, Tkac identifies the proliferation of different types of funds and the recent emergence of the funds' main competitor, the ETF, as among the more important developments in the fund industry. She adds to that list the provision by fund sponsors of other services apart from the funds themselves: information, investment advice, planning, recordkeeping, and access to and trading of other investment products. Indeed, she notes that in 2005 more of the people working in the fund industry serviced investors' accounts than managed fund portfolios.

The structure of the fund industry as well as the way that funds are distributed have changed in significant respects. Thirty years ago, funds generally were sold through brokers, who were paid out of a front-end load, or sales charge. With the adoption of rule 12b-1 in 1980 by the Securities and Exchange Commission, mutual funds were allowed to spread their marketing and distribution charges out over time and to take the costs out of fund assets. Tkac notes that many fund companies implemented the rule by introducing new share classes within the same fund, with each share class having its own fee structure. That, in turn, enabled fund advisers to distribute shares in various ways: through captive brokers, wholesalers, and financial advisers; through institutional pension or 401(k) programs; and to investors directly.

Perhaps the most important change in fund distribution in the past fifteen years in particular was the development of "open architecture" or "open platform" methods of distribution. Under this approach, fund sponsors give investors access to a range of funds, including those offered and managed by other advisers. Much of industry thus has moved away from a specialist, proprietary structure and toward "financial supermarkets" that offer investors a broad choice of funds as well as a range of investment-related services.

Looking ahead, Tkac predicts that the most important factor affecting fund investment activity and patterns will be the retirement of the baby boom generation. Up to this point, of course, baby boomers have fueled the increase in assets invested in funds, encouraged by the shift among employers from defined benefit to defined contribution retirement plans, in which most of the funds are invested in mutual funds. Now that the baby boomers are beginning to retire, they will withdraw from rather than add to their fund accounts. In such an environment, a key challenge for fund companies will be to offset as best they can those withdrawals with new deposits from younger investors. At the same time, fund companies should find new service opportunities in advising retirees on how to draw down ("decumulate") their fund balances, as some companies already are doing through the "retirement calculators" featured on their websites.

In her chapter, Tkac surveys various theories about how retirees can best make the difficult decisions involved in "asset decumulation." Key factors in the decision include their tolerance for risk—specifically, the risk that they might outlive their assets—and the extent to which they want to leave bequests to their heirs. One obvious way for individuals to reduce or even eliminate longevity risk is by purchasing annuities. While the current annuity market is small, Tkac suggests that insurers that offer annuities will become more innovative in their attempts to spur demand for this particular investment product in the future.

Tkac expects fund sponsors to build on their past record of innovation in their efforts to attract investments from younger workers. In particular, Tkac predicts that mutual fund companies will broaden the range of their offerings of other financial services and increase their use of Internet technologies to refine and individualize the investment products and services that they offer to investors.

The Mutual Fund Industry in Japan

In the United States, mutual funds are organized legally as "investment companies," which technically are corporations, whose shares represent the prorated market value of the assets held by the funds. Mutual fund owners thus are "shareholders," who elect the members of the fund's board of directors, which oversees the operation of the funds. The investment strategy of the funds, however, is set by an investment adviser, who typically has organized and marketed the funds.

In Japan, as in some other countries, the more popular mutual funds are those that have been organized instead as investment trusts, which are administered by a fund trustee without a board of directors overseeing the fund. Investors in investment funds have a contractual rather than a shareholder relationship with their funds.

In chapter 2, Koichi Iwai of the Nomura Institute of Capital Markets Research examines the growth of investment trusts in Japan and offers his views about the future. Japanese investors have been slower to embrace their equivalent of mutual funds than investors in the United States, although that has been changing. Inflows into investment trusts were substantial in the late 1980s, just before Japan's stock market "bubble" burst, and in the past few years they again have become significant. During the 1990s—Japan's "lost decade"—Japanese investors pulled their money out of investment trusts.

Given the popularity of foreign currency–denominated mutual funds, Iwai postulates that inflows into Japanese trusts should react positively to yen weakening (which makes Japanese securities more attractive). In addition, fund inflows should increase as equity returns widen relative to interest rates on savings deposits. Iwai presents a statistical study that confirms both hypotheses. Of particular interest, he reports that exchange rate movements have had a greater impact on net fund inflows since 2003 than beforehand.

Iwai points to two regulatory changes affecting the distribution of investment trusts in Japan that he believes also have stimulated inflows into the trusts. One change allowed banks (in 1998) and later the post office (in 2005) to sell shares in investment trusts. The second change, adopted in 2001, introduced defined contribution pension plans. Five years later, in 2006, investment trusts accounted for nearly 40 percent of the assets in those plans.

Product innovation also has led to growing interest in investment trusts among Japanese investors. Iwai notes that interest in investment trusts rises with age and that Japanese investors tend to be risk averse and more interested in obtaining regular income than capital gains from their trusts. Hence, trust investors have been most interested in balanced funds (which pay dividends), funds of funds, and foreign currency–denominated funds.

Iwai advances a short-run projection for the growth of investment trust assets in Japan. Using existing trust investment tendencies by age cohort and taking account of the positive relationship between investor age and the amount of funds invested in trusts, Iwai projects that because of the continued aging of the Japanese population, total investment trust assets should be 45 percent higher in 2010 than in 2000.

Looking out over a longer time horizon, Iwai identifies a number of factors that, unless they change, should limit the growth of the investment trust industry. One such factor relates to the "default choice" for individuals enrolled in contribution plans. For most workers, the current default is a savings account. Unless that changes, the opportunities for further growth in pension monies allocated to investment trusts will be capped. A second factor limiting the growth of assets is the greater concentration—and thus less intense competition—that exists in the Japanese fund industry than in the U.S. industry. A third limiting factor is that Japanese financial organizations tend to favor trusts advised by their own asset managers, a tendency confirmed by Iwai's empirical analysis. That tendency, which effectively limits customer choice and thus possibly interest in trust investments generally, contrasts with the movement toward the open architecture distribution model for mutual funds in the United States.

Finally, the growth of the investment trust industry is limited by the current preference of Japanese investors for income-oriented investment vehicles. Investor education about the benefits of investing in growth-oriented vehicles would expand the horizons of Japanese investors and thus widen opportunities for the growth of investment trusts in the future.

Mutual Funds in Europe and Elsewhere

As suggested by the total amount of assets noted previously, the mutual fund industry has become a global phenomenon. As of year-end 2006, assets held in mutual funds outside the United States exceeded the assets of U.S. funds. What lies ahead for mutual funds around the world? Ajay Khorana of the Georgia Institute of Technology and Henri Servaes of the London Business School address a number of aspects of this question in chapter 3.

Khorana and Servaes begin with a brief survey of the fund industry around the world. Notably, although fund assets are largest in the United States, relative to national output (GDP), the ratio of fund assets to GDP is next highest in Luxembourg, followed closely by Ireland. Both countries have become hubs for fund sales throughout Europe.

Looking ahead, the authors suggest that an important precondition for rapid growth in fund assets in a country is that fund assets relative to GDP be relatively low, so that ample room exists for future growth. Once that condition is met, growth should depend heavily on the quality of a country's legal system. For that reason, although the ratio of fund assets to GDP is small in countries such as China, India, Russia, and Turkey, fund growth in those countries is likely to be limited unless the quality of their legal systems improves significantly. Other factors that also should influence the rate of growth of fund assets are the ease and cost of forming new funds and the prevalence of defined contribution plans, which are major sources of fund asset growth.

Mutual funds are sold through three channels: directly by fund management companies, through financial advisers, and by commercial banks. Khorana and

Servaes expect no major changes in current distribution patterns. However, they do report evidence indicating that financial advisers do not benefit investors but instead tend to raise fees and reduce risk-adjusted returns.

Not all countries have a "free market" in the sale of mutual funds—that is, they do not permit funds established in foreign countries to be sold in the domestic market. That is the case in Australia, Canada, Japan, and the United States, but there are significant cross-border mutual fund sales in Europe. The authors do not expect major changes in existing patterns, although they do anticipate some decline in European sales from Luxembourg and Ireland as European governments make it more difficult to hide ownership and income from funds in the two countries. Further, with the expiration of the tax advantages that helped spur the growth of the fund industry in Ireland, the authors expect Luxembourg to widen its lead over Ireland in future growth of fund assets on the Continent.

Khorana and Servaes also address certain of the controversial issues related to mutual fund fees, which are of two broad types: fees assessed when investors buy or sell fund shares and fees assessed annually (for portfolio management and, in some places, to pay for fund distribution and marketing). Fees vary significantly across and within countries, even when adjusted for size of funds, but as a percentage of assets, they typically go down as funds get larger and are able to realize economies of scale. By the authors' calculations, fund fees are lowest in Australia and highest in Canada. Fees in the United States are relatively modest compared with those in other countries. Fee-related lawsuits filed in the United States against fund companies so far have not succeeded, although the authors suggest that there may be downward pressure on fees if plaintiffs begin to prevail in such suits.

The authors note that one type of fee—the "performance-based" fee—is much more common in Europe than in the United States. Such fees are imposed if and when performance exceeds some benchmark. Performance fees are not common in the United States, because by law any such fees must be symmetric—if they rise for good performance, they must fall for poor performance. In Europe, however, fund managers can charge performance fees that are asymmetric—fees can go up if funds outpace the benchmark but do not have to go down if they fall below it. The authors note that performance fees are charged by 12 percent of European equity funds and suggest that use of such fees in Europe (but not the United States) will be more frequent in the future.

As we noted at the outset, the diversity of mutual funds has been growing over time. Khorana and Servaes single out several fund categories that have become increasingly popular in recent years and that they expect to become even more so in the future: index funds; guaranteed funds (funds established for a fixed period that increase in value if a specific index rises and guarantee the return of principal should the index not increase in value over that period); funds that specialize in certain industry sectors; and hedged mutual funds (funds that follow investment strategies similar to those of hedge funds). The authors are more cautious about the future of "funds of funds"—mutual funds that invest in other mutual funds—because of the multiple layers of fees embedded in such funds.

Khorana and Servaes also present an extensive discussion of the behavior of mutual fund investors. Specifically, they ask whether investors tend to act rationally, seeking to maximize the risk-adjusted, after-tax returns of their funds, net of fees. The authors identify several patterns of investor behavior suggesting that the answer to that question is no.

One such pattern shows that fund investors tend to chase fund "winners"— funds that have performed the best over some recent time period or those that have been rated the best by independent rating services such as Morningstar. The best study of this "hot hand" phenomenon, however, suggests that investors' faith in recent winners is misplaced: past returns are not a statistically valid predictor of future returns, except in the case of poorly performing funds, which consistently tend to perform poorly. The exception for poor performers highlights a second oddity: that despite the funds' persistent poor performance, investors in such funds do not consistently withdraw their money beyond the first "bad year."

A third pattern inconsistent with the rational actor model is the persistence of large differences in fees among funds of the same type, such as index funds. In a rational world, such differences would not persist—investors would flock to the fund or funds with the lowest expense ratios—but Khorana and Servaes indicate that so far, they have not. Further, although all fees come out of investors' pockets and ideally should affect fund flows in the same fashion, in fact investors tend to pay more attention to fees that are more transparent, such as front-end load or sales charges, than to annual expenses.

The authors suggest that fund sponsors can take advantage of these oddities in investor behavior by promoting their best-performing funds (if the sponsors offer a "family" of fund choices), by increasing their fees across the board (as long as the fees remain below average and thus do not tend to stick out in any fee comparison chart), and by offering and promoting guaranteed funds (which are relatively inexpensive to manage because they tend to be linked to indexes).

Khorana and Servaes also highlight recent academic research exploring the characteristics that seem to be associated with successful fund management (management that results in risk-adjusted returns that are better than relevant benchmarks). Two manager-specific characteristics stand out: average SAT score at the college that the managers attended and the amount of personal wealth invested by the managers in the funds that they manage, both of which seem to be positively related to fund performance. The authors cite one study suggesting that fund returns tend to fall with fund size but rise as the size of a fund's family (the other funds offered by the same sponsor) increases. They note another line of research indicating that fund performance goes up with portfolio concentration, indicating that a few big bets may pay off better than many smaller ones.

The authors conclude by observing that there are large numbers of fund sponsors, around the world and within individual countries. Nonetheless, in the United States and elsewhere, the collective market share of the largest fund companies has been relatively stable. That pattern suggests the presence of economies of scale, which, in the authors' view, should lead to some consolidation among fund sponsors in the years ahead. The authors project that this trend will enhance the profitability of the surviving fund sponsors rather than result in savings to investors.

Commenters' Views

This book closes with four comments relating to the future of mutual funds: one comment by Brian Reid of the Investment Company Institute (ICI) on the contrasts in the conclusions and arguments of the chapter by Tkac and the chapter by Khorana and Servaes and three comments on the future of mutual fund regulation.

In Tkac's view, demographic characteristics—especially age of the investor—are the driving force behind fund investment and the force to which profit-maximizing fund sponsors respond. Khorana and Servaes agree that profit-maximization guides the behavior of fund sponsors, but they are skeptical that fund investors act in a rational fashion

Reid rejects the view that investors are not rational, while agreeing that demographic trends should have an important effect on the fund industry in the future. He points to evidence from the ICI showing much greater relative inflows into low-fee funds than those charging higher fees. Reid argues that that evidence, coupled with investors' stated desire for financial services that offer more than just the option of buying and selling mutual funds, suggests that funds charging higher fees are meeting investor demand for other services. Reid notes that nevertheless, on balance and for stock funds in particular, the ratio of fees to assets invested has declined by a little more than half since 1980, a decline that in his view is consistent with investors' paying attention to fees.

Looking ahead, Reid expects fund companies to continue to innovate and specifically to address demand for a broader range of financial services as many investors retire. He singles out the new "target date" funds, which are meeting investor demand for a convenient investment vehicle that is well suited to retirement needs, and suggests that such funds should play an important role in the future growth of the fund industry, at least in the United States. In addition, like Tkac, Reid expects continued innovation by fund companies to respond to the decumulation of fund assets as baby boomers retire. He also forecasts the squeezing of fund companies' margins, which in turn should lead to further consolidation.

In the United States, mutual funds are regulated by the Securities and Exchange Commission, under provisions of the Investment Company Act of 1940 and subsequent amendments. The 1940 act requires fund sponsors to make various kinds of disclosures and vests responsibility for oversight in boards of directors to prevent fund managers from exploiting conflicts of interest. The other discussants—Peter Wallison of the American Enterprise Institute, Allan Mostoff of the Mutual Fund Directors Forum, and Harold Bradley of the Kauffman Foundation—comment on how the regulatory environment may change in the future.

Wallison contends that the structure of the mutual fund industry, the result of federal regulations that promote boards of directors and a corporate structure, is inhibiting competition. Citing evidence that compares fee dispersion in the United States and the United Kingdom, Wallison attributes the much wider fee distribution in the United States to disincentives for boards of directors to reduce fees. To increase industry competition in the future, he advocates moving away from structuring mutual funds as corporations. Instead, the law should permit funds to be organized (on an optional basis) as they are in many European countries—and somewhat as they are in Japan—as trusts whose portfolios are managed by a trustee (or an equivalent) without a board of directors.

Mostoff, in contrast, argues that boards of directors are a crucial and beneficial component of the mutual fund industry. In his view, boards help maintain and enhance investors' trust in funds, which is indispensable for their future growth. Mostoff acknowledges that boards have not always been perfect but argues that they offer the most cost-effective means of oversight.

Bradley, who has spent numerous decades working in the mutual fund industry, approaches regulatory issues from the perspective of an insider. He notes that although fee structures may be problematic, mutual funds still offer the lowest-cost method for the average investor to achieve diversification and benefit from portfolio management and advice. Fees, however, are still being set by a few industry players, and in his view they are less than transparent. A key object of regulation in the years ahead, therefore, should be to enhance transparency.

Conclusion

The mutual fund industry has enjoyed spectacular growth in the United States and elsewhere since the end of World War II. Funds have offered a cost-effective way for investors to diversity their assets. As investors age, earn more, and grow wealthier, they have put more of their assets into funds or equivalent vehicles.

The fund industry will be challenged in the years ahead by the retirement of the post–World War II generation of workers, especially in developed countries. If the past is any guide to the future, however, fund companies will continue to innovate to meet new needs. And debate will continue over how mutual funds are best governed. The chapters in this book shed light on each of these important issues.

PAULA A. TKAC 1

Mutual Fund Innovation: Past and Future

The only thing that stays the same is change.

—HERACLITUS/MELISSA ETHERIDGE

THE PROCESS OF change, whether in technology, marketing, or the mutual fund industry, is continual. As the demands of investors change and new intellectual discoveries are made, new technology becomes available, and new regulations are passed, the marketplace changes and mutual fund families are presented with new opportunities to make a profit. Innovation, then, is both certain and at the same time unpredictable. It is easy to predict that change will occur—for nothing stays the same—but it is very difficult to predict the exact form that innovation will take.[1] The goal of this chapter, nonetheless, is to predict future innovations in the mutual fund industry.

In predicting the future, it helps to look to the past. Studying previous innovations increases understanding of the economic forces and motivations that currently influence mutual fund families, financial advisers, and investors. That knowledge, combined with basic economic analysis, is the key to predicting how those players will change and react to change in the future. It also helps to have a

1. That reflects the proverbial $20 bill on the sidewalk problem: the obviously profitable innovations already have been undertaken.

predictable, exogenous event that will quite certainly affect the industry. Fortunately, we are in the middle of just such an event right now—the unstoppable progression toward retirement of the baby boom generation.

The baby boom has been affecting the U.S. economy since it began in 1946. *Newsweek* magazine reported on the birthrate increase in 1948 in an article entitled "Population: Babies Mean Business," which chronicled the rising demand for infant clothing and prepared baby food and noted the new firms starting up in the children's recording and book industries. Moreover, the article noted, "business analysts predicted that eventually the boom in babies would have salutary effects on every corner of the nation's economy."[2] The mutual fund industry has been no exception. Mutual funds have, almost literally, grown up with the baby boomers, and the shift of the 80 million members of that generation from worker-savers to retirees-consumers will surely influence the evolution of the industry going forward. This chapter presents an analysis of some of the likely features of future changes.

Financial Innovation in the Mutual Fund Industry

In considering how the U.S. mutual fund industry is likely to evolve in the future, it is instructive to take a brief look at industry innovations in the recent past. A comprehensive look at the process and drivers of financial innovation, even within the mutual fund world, is beyond the scope of this chapter, but Tufano (2003) and Frame and White (2004) provide modern surveys of the academic literature regarding financial innovation more broadly. As those studies note, innovation can involve the introduction of new financial products or services, new or enhanced processes for developing or distributing products and services, and new organizational forms. Innovation in behind-the-scenes processes such as recordkeeping and quantitative modeling will not, for the most part, be addressed in this chapter, but it surely is occurring nonetheless. The pages that follow provide a "helicopter tour" of innovations in products, services, and industry organization in the mutual fund industry as well as a brief discussion of the forces driving the innovations.

Product Innovations

The 8,120 mutual funds in existence today, defined broadly as open-end commingled accounts, have already been the subject of much innovation; many in fact are quite different from the original fund, the Massachusetts Investors Trust (MIT), introduced in 1924. Still in existence more than eighty years later, MIT

2. "Population: Babies Mean Business," *Newsweek*, August 9, 1948, pp. 21–23.

is what we would today call an actively managed domestic equity growth and income fund. A major type of innovation in mutual funds has been to extend the product to include portfolios in other asset classes, including all types of bonds (corporate, municipal, high-yield), international equities and debt, and short-term money market instruments. Moreover, there is now a language to describe the "style" of mutual fund portfolios. Mutual funds are commonly categorized by the capitalization (small, mid-cap, large) and the growth orientation (growth, value, blend) of their holdings. The 1980s saw the introduction of a variety of sector funds, allowing investors access to portfolios comprising stocks in a particular industry, such as energy, health care, technology, or dotcoms. This array of more narrowly defined mutual fund styles has expanded investor opportunities by allowing investors to custom design their overall investment allocations while retaining the benefits of cost-efficient diversification and fund management within each segment.

Two more recent innovations in that vein include the introduction of socially responsible mutual funds and the very new 130/30 funds.[3] Socially responsible funds allow investors to structure their portfolios in accordance with their personal goals for both financial gain and social action. Entry into this market has largely been led by smaller advisory firms that specialize in socially responsible investing (for example, Calvert and Domini), but several large advisory firms—such as Fidelity, TIAA-CREF, and AXA—also added a few socially responsible funds to their lineup. The 130/30 funds and other long-short funds differ from traditional long-only equity funds in that they leverage their long investments by short selling a fraction of the value of the portfolio, in this case 30 percent. That general strategy, which has been a common practice in hedge fund portfolios, has diffused into the retail fund market, most likely because of its good results.

Some mutual fund innovation has focused more on the investment process than on the type of portfolio holdings. In 1976 John C. Bogle introduced the first passively managed index fund offered to retail investors.[4] Following on academic research that suggested that a market index portfolio not only was optimal from a theoretical point of view but also was likely to earn higher returns than most actively managed mutual funds, index funds gave investors access to a diversified portfolio of stocks without the risk that the portfolio manager was in actuality quite unskilled at picking stocks. Since that time, the menu of index funds has grown to include passively managed funds in every style and asset class.

3. In March 2006, Morningstar introduced a new long-short category for funds that maintain a 20 percent short position over a multiyear period.
4. In 1971 Wells Fargo introduced an equally weighted S&P 500 index fund, sold through private placement.

A concept similar to the automatic portfolio allocations of index funds lies behind the very new lifecycle (or target date) funds. Academic research provided validation for a policy of shifting portfolio weights from equities to bonds as an investor ages.[5] Lifecycle funds automate the reallocation, thus saving investors time and effort and thereby creating value. These funds have been very popular since their introduction in 1995. In 2006 they had amassed $114 billion in assets under management, with roughly 90 percent of those assets held in retirement accounts.[6]

Finally, one of the largest and most successful innovations in mutual fund investing has been the introduction of a new type of investment fund: exchange-traded funds (ETFs).[7] ETFs are similar to index funds in that they are passively managed to duplicate the return on an index. In that respect, ETFs certainly are substitutes for open-end index mutual funds for many investors, but they remain distinct because they have a single distribution channel. Unlike mutual funds, which can be purchased directly from a fund company or through an adviser or a broker, ETFs are sold exclusively through brokers and trade on an exchange like shares of stock. Since their introduction in 1993, the evolution of ETFs has mimicked that of mutual funds in general. In 2006 alone, sixty-seven new industry or sector ETFs were launched and total net assets in ETFs reached $422 billion,[8] spread across both equity and fixed-income and domestic and international asset classes. The growth in ETFs has been driven by both individual and institutional investors.

Figures 1-1a and 1-1b show the growth in the number and assets of the more recent mutual fund innovations: lifecycle funds, ETFs, lifestyle funds, and funds of funds. Lifestyle funds maintain a specific risk level over time (for example, aggressive or conservative). Funds of funds are mutual funds comprising shares in other mutual funds; they include both lifecycle and lifestyle funds, along with funds pursuing a multimanager style.

Advice and Services

Perhaps the greatest innovation in mutual funds is that they have progressed from being investment vehicles for the most part to including various bundles of investor services, including provision of information and investment advice, planning, recordkeeping, and access to and trading of other investment products. In 2005 the ICI *Mutual Fund Factbook* reported that investor services accounted for

5. See Bodie, Merton, and Samuelson (1992).
6. Investment Company Institute, *Mutual Fund Factbook 2007* (www.icifactbook.org/ICI).
7. For a thorough history of ETFs and their predecessors, see Gastineau (2002).
8. Investment Company Institute, *Mutual Fund Factbook 2007*, section 43 (www.icifactbook.org/ICI).

Figure 1-1a. *Total Net Assets in Four Innovative Products, 1989–2006*

Dollars (millions)

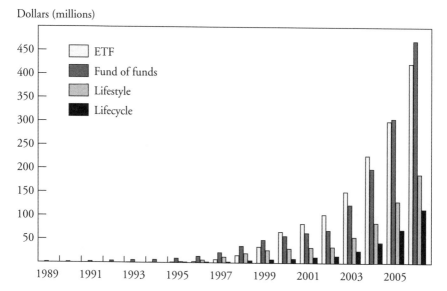

Figure 1-1b. *Number of Funds in Four Innovative Products, 1989–2006*

Number

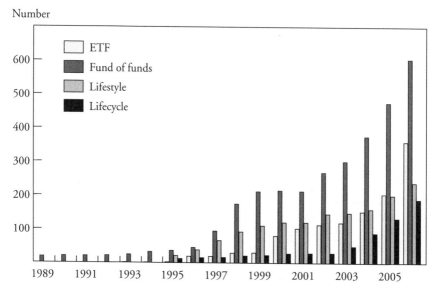

Source: Investment Company Institute, *Mutual Fund Factbook 2007*, data tables, sections 3 and 5.

a larger percentage of jobs in registered investment companies than fund management (32 percent versus 31 percent). If sales and distribution employees are included as providers of investor services of some type, the percentage increases to 55 percent of employees. While there are no readily accessible data for earlier periods, it seems reasonable to assume that the fraction of employees involved in fund management was much greater in past decades.

Within the last decade the list of investor services has grown to include Internet access to enhanced versions of all services, plus real time account management. An especially powerful way to observe this facet of service evolution is to compare the website of a major mutual fund advisory firm, Fidelity Investments, in 1997 with its website today.[9] For example, in 1997 Fidelity's site map easily fit on one computer screen, while the 2007 version included roughly four screens of links to various products and services. In addition to innovations in online account access, the 2007 website provided information and services related to active trading, investment products such as insurance and annuities, and information and advice on planning for college, estate planning, charitable giving, and taxes and tax strategies.

While a comparison of the websites illustrates advances in web design over the past decade, the tremendous growth in these online tools, research, and advice also is apparent. Moreover, fund families are actively advertising their advice in addition to their fund return performance. In a recent web ad for Vanguard, for example, an array of neckties in a myriad of patterns and colors scrolls by, along with a question: "Need help choosing?" The analogy to selecting investment products is clear, and the main service being promoted is Vanguard's ability to help investors make good decisions.

Improvements in investment information and advice also come from firms outside the investment management industry. Examples are information intermediaries such as Lipper and Morningstar, founded in 1973 and 1984, respectively, and financial media publishers such as Smartmoney, founded in 1997. Today these firms and others provide everything from basic fund information to sophisticated analytics and planning tools to both individual and institutional investors and financial advisers. Mutual fund investors value objective and easy-to-interpret information on the performance of funds and how they compare with others, such as that presented by the Morningstar star-rating system, because it significantly reduces decisionmaking costs in terms of both time and effort. The continued survival of information intermediaries is a testament to the value that

---

9. The current Fidelity website can be accessed at http://personal.fidelity.com/accounts/services/index_sitemap.html?refhp=pr; the 1997 Fidelity website can be accessed through the Way Back Machine at http://web.archive.org/web/19970126072646/www.fidelity.com/misc/sitemap/sitemap.html.

investors place on their services.[10] These firms also continued to innovate: Morningstar revised its star-rating algorithm to include style categories in 2002 and introduced fund governance-stewardship ratings following the mutual fund market-timing scandal in 2003.

Industry Structure

The organization and structure of the mutual fund industry also have changed over time. Before 1980, mutual funds were either sold through brokers, who were compensated through front-end load fees, or sold directly to investors with no load fee. In 1980 the SEC approved rule 12b-1, which allowed funds to spread distribution and marketing fees out over time. Mutual funds implemented the rule through the introduction of new share classes within one mutual fund, with each share class having its own fee structure. The ability to offer multiple share classes allowed fund advisers to distribute shares through different channels—captive brokers, wholesalers, financial advisers, and institutional 401(k) programs—and they also could sell directly to investors. The use of share classes has been quite popular. In 2006, for example, 21,260 share classes were offered, representing 8,120 unique mutual fund portfolios, for an average of 2.6 share classes per fund.[11]

Investors participate in these channels according to their preferences for advice and service and the availability of employer-based investment opportunities. The proliferation of share classes and the consequent spread in distribution has made it more and more difficult to pigeonhole a mutual fund firm into any one distribution channel, resulting in the characterization of today's market as suffering from "channel blur."[12] Thus 12b-1 fees have given mutual fund advisers a convenient way to reach different types of investors. While I believe that this change has been beneficial, it is worth noting that the process of expanding access across distribution channels would likely have occurred without 12b-1 fees, albeit in different ways.

Another way in which mutual fund advisers have broadened their investor bases is through the increasing use of subadvisory contracts.[13] Subadvisory contracts are

10. Confirming that "market test," Del Guercio and Tkac (forthcoming) documents that changes in Morningstar ratings have a significant and in some cases quite large effect on the flow of investment into specific funds.

11. Investment Company Institute, *Mutual Fund Factbook 2007*, data tables, section 1, table 1 (www.icifactbook.org/ICI).

12. Data on distribution channels from Financial Research Corporation (FRC) indicate that the percentage of mutual fund advisers with more than 75 percent of their assets distributed through one channel fell from 91 percent to 74 percent between 1996 and 2002.

13. The discussion of subadvisory contracts is based on Del Guercio, Reuter, and Tkac (2007), which includes an analysis of the economics of subadvisory contracts and statistics on this practice.

essentially outsourcing arrangements between mutual fund advisers and other portfolio management firms (institutional asset managers and other mutual fund advisers). In effect, the contracts allow subadvisers to profit from managing a portfolio that ultimately is distributed through a channel that the subadvisers would find unprofitable to serve on their own. Over the period 1996–2006, the trend was toward greater use of subadvisory contracts (by 7 percent of funds in 1996, 12 percent in 2002, and 17 percent in 2006), and mutual fund advisers have been serving as subadvisers with increasing frequency. Thirty-four percent of subadvisory contracts in 1996 involved mutual fund subadvisers; the share grew to 52 percent in 2002.[14] A closer analysis reveals that mutual fund firms serve as subadvisers almost exclusively for funds distributed through channels that are different from their own (for example, a firm that sells mutual funds directly will subadvise for an adviser that sells funds through a captive broker). Subadvisory contracts have also been used to facilitate entry into the mutual fund market by other financial service providers, such as ING, and insurance companies like Pacific Life. These firms employ a "virtual family" strategy in which they employ subadvisers for all of their funds, lowering the cost and development time required to bring mutual fund offerings to their investors.

A related development in the past fifteen years has been the shift from proprietary fund distribution to the open architecture of fund supermarkets. In 1992 Schwab OneSource became the first retail mutual fund supermarket, providing Schwab investors access to a variety of funds run by other fund advisers. Since that time, several other brokers and large fund families have offered supermarkets to their investors, including ETrade, TD Ameritrade, Vanguard, Fidelity, and T. Rowe Price. As of 2004, an estimated $600 billion in mutual fund assets was held through supermarket arrangements.[15] The motivation to participate in supermarkets is similar to that for the subadvisory market: supermarkets allow families such as Dodge & Cox to access Fidelity's distribution channel and provides investors with a wider scope of products.

Along with subadvising and the enhancement of investor services, the existence of cross-selling through supermarkets suggests the primacy of "client accounts" in the economic calculus of mutual fund advisory firms. It does not seem a stretch to characterize mutual fund families as having morphed from small shops specializing in the stock-picking ability of their managers to large-scale financial service firms that provide a range of products and services to meet the

14. Del Guercio, Reuter, and Tkac (2007).
15. Laura Sanders, "Supermarket Sweepstakes," Forbes, September 20, 2004.

multidimensional demands of their customers.[16] Surely, portfolio management is still the core product, but it is now packaged with services to increase investor confidence, peace of mind, and satisfaction with respect to risk, planning, and safety.

Drivers of Innovation

Mutual funds are in many ways no different from many other goods and services produced and consumed in the United States. In all industries, firms seek to maximize profits, which, in turn, motivates them to decrease the costs of production or distribution, increase the value of output to consumers, and create valuable new products and services to sell to new groups of consumers. And that motivation spurs innovation—making changes in the production process, developing new products, marketing new uses for existing products, and so forth.

At the heart of every innovation is a new, profitable, creative idea. It is difficult, if not impossible, to speak of the cause of innovation since there is no observable font from which new ideas spring, fully formed. Furthermore, as Tufano (2003) notes, it is likely incorrect to attribute any particular innovation to one cause alone. However, a look at past innovations helps to characterize some of the forces that seem to have driven them.

In some cases, innovations occurred largely without any change in the external market environment. For example, academic research on fund management and performance provided a strong conceptual base for development of index funds and lifecycle funds and likely for the advent of style-based investing (that is, drawing on return anomalies documented in the academic literature). Innovations in industry structure, like subadvising and fund supermarkets, typically diffuse throughout the industry without a particular impetus—one firm identifies a profitable new strategy and others mimic it as they assess their own profit opportunities. Other innovations are strongly influenced by discrete changes in nonmarket factors such as regulation or tax policy. Examples are the introduction of share classes as described above and advice regarding the tax efficiency of various funds and other investment products.

Many innovations occur in response to or are aided by changes in the market environment in which mutual fund families operate. For example, there is no doubt that technological advances have contributed substantially to almost all of the product and service innovations described earlier by decreasing the cost of

---

16. To be sure, there are many smaller, boutique fund shops remaining, but the majority of industry assets and flows accrue to the larger, multidimensional fund families.

computation and memory and by making it possible to disseminate information and account services over the Internet. The remainder of this chapter looks into the future, toward fundamental changes in the preferences of and the decisions facing the investor base of mutual fund families and the industry innovations that are likely to follow.

Looking to the Future: Demographic Changes

While it often is impossible to predict where and how innovation will occur in the mutual fund industry, sometimes changes in the underlying economic environment are significant enough to provide a glimpse of the industry's potential future. The movement of the baby boomers into retirement is an example—a fundamental change in investor demographics is on the horizon, predictable enough that it has already motivated innovation in mutual funds and is likely to spur even more.

The baby boom generation typically is defined as the roughly 80 million people born in the United States between 1948 and 1964. During that period the fertility rate increased from 2.3 children per woman in 1940 to 3.3 children per woman at the peak of the boom in 1957.[17] Since that time, the fertility rate has dropped back down to a roughly stable 2.05. The resulting effect on the age distribution of the U.S. population in 1985 is illustrated in figure 1-2a, where the baby boom is seen as the bulge between ages 20 and 40. That bulge in the population distribution moves predictably, inexorably, to the right as time passes; it still can be identified in 2006 (figure 1-2b). Using projections from the U.S. Census Bureau based on current trends in fertility, mortality, and immigration, figure 1-2c is a snapshot of what the population distribution is likely to look like in 2025. The baby boom is still reflected in the relatively higher proportion of people between 60 and 80 years of age. However, the bulge is not as apparent—the population distribution is projected to be much flatter than it was twenty years ago. That is the result of two main effects—the positive relation between mortality rate and age (natural attrition at the top end of the distribution) and higher levels of immigration of individuals at the younger end of the distribution than existed in earlier periods.

While the retirement of the baby boomers is the central focus of this chapter, the growth of the younger portion of the population is important as well. Figure 1-3 illustrates the number of people in the age ranges 25–39, 40–64, and 65 and above over the period 1980–2025, using projections for future dates. Those age groups correspond roughly to three different investor clienteles: young workers, traditional

17. See Simon and Tamura (2007).

Figure 1-2. *U.S. Population Distribution, 1985, 2006, 2025*

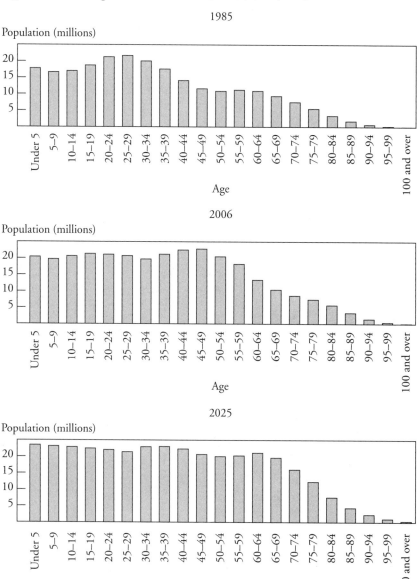

Source: U.S. Bureau of the Census. Projected data can be found at www.census.gov/population/ www/
projections/popproj.html; historical data (prior) to 2006 can be found at www.census.gov/compendia/
statab/hist_stats.html and www.census.gov/compendia/statab/cats/population.html.

Figure 1-3. *U.S. Population, by Age Group, 1980–2025*

Population (millions)

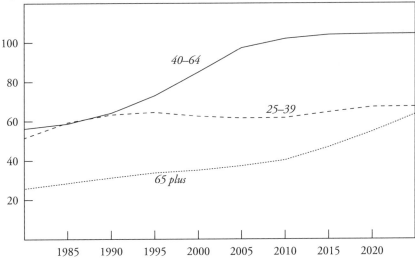

Source: U.S. Bureau of the Census. Projected data can be found at www.census.gov/population/www/ projections/popproj.html; historical data (prior) to 2006 can be found at www.census.gov/compendia/ statab/hist_stats.html and www.census.gov/compendia/statab/cats/population.html.

savers, and retirees. According to a Fidelity Investments survey, traditional savers have an average personal savings rate of 4.3 percent and are in their prime wealth accumulation years, saving for both college and retirement.[18] Young workers, in contrast, have a personal savings rate of only 2.9 percent despite a median pre-tax income that is only $5,000 less than that of traditional savers. While the retiree group is projected to be the fastest growing over the next twenty years, the largest number of potential investors will be traditional savers (that is, those who are young workers now). That represents a significant market opportunity for mutual fund families.

Several trends already have affected and will continue to affect the financial opportunities and decisions of baby boomers as they face the prospect of retirement:

—*The shift from defined benefit to defined contribution employer-sponsored retire-ment plans.* Over the past twenty years, the percentage of private sector workers participating in defined benefit plans dropped from 80 percent to 33 percent

18. Kathie O'Donnell, "GenXers Lag in Retirement Savings," *Investment News,* March 26, 2007.

while the percentage of employees with defined contribution plans increased from 41 percent to 51 percent.[19] In terms of assets, currently $4.1 trillion in retirement savings is held in defined contribution plans while only $2.3 trillion is held in defined benefit plans.[20] That change means that workers are now—and will be in the future—much more responsible for managing their own financial plans for retirement than prior generations were. The stable source of retirement income offered by defined benefit plans has been replaced by a system in which workers guide both the accumulation and decumulation of savings. The majority of defined contribution assets are held in mutual funds, and the shift of risk from employers to workers has spurred much of the demand for and subsequent growth of investment advice.

—*Increasing life expectancy.* In 1960 life expectancy for a baby born that year was 69.7 years; for a person turning 65 in 1960, life expectancy was 14.3 more years. Both of those statistics have increased in the past forty-five years: a child born in 2004 had a life expectancy of 77.8 years, and a person who was 65 years old in 2004 could expect to live another 18.7 years.[21] As baby boomers have aged, their projected lifetimes have increased. Assuming a constant retirement age of 65 years combined with the trend toward defined contribution retirement plans implies that over time investors are facing the prospect of funding longer retirements than their parents or grandparents did.

—*Social Security insolvency.* According to the 2007 *Social Security Trust Fund Report,* Social Security tax revenues will be insufficient to fund outlays beginning in 2017. By 2041, the government will be able to fund only 75 percent of projected benefits with tax revenues. The trust fund report estimates that an immediate increase in payroll taxes of 16 percent or a 13 percent reduction in benefits would bring the program into actuarial balance.[22] Given the Bush administration's failed attempt to reform Social Security and introduce private accounts in 2005 and the upcoming 2008 presidential elections, no immediate action to address the Social Security funding shortfall is likely to be taken. The longer the underfunding remains unaddressed, the larger the ultimate changes in taxes or benefits will have to be. According to a 2007 AXA Equitable survey, 86 percent

19. Statistics for 1985 and 2003, respectively, for workers who participate in a retirement plan. From the *Employee Benefits Research Institute Factbook 2007* (www.ebri.org/publications/books/index.cfm? fa=databook).

20. Investment Company Institute, *Mutual Fund Factbook 2007* (www.icifactbook.org/ICI).

21. All of these statistics are from the Centers for Disease Control and Prevention, Department of Health and Human Services (www.cdc.gov/nchs/).

22. *Social Securities Trust Fund Report 2007* (www.treas.gov/offices/economic-policy/reports/social-security-report-2007.pdf).

of workers surveyed believed that reform would include an increase in the age at which benefits were paid and 73 percent predicted a reduction in benefits.[23] That implies that future retirees will be exposed to both a decline in expected benefits and significant uncertainty regarding the actual level of the Social Security benefits, if any, that they are likely to receive.

—*Health care costs and the Medicare crisis.* When it comes to Medicare, the funding situation is similar to that with Social Security, but more dire.[24] Medicare costs are expected to surpass Social Security expenditures in 2028 due to the continuing high rate of increase in health care costs. By 2019, the Medicare Hospital Insurance Trust Fund will be able to fund only 79 percent of expenditures from tax receipts. Not surprisingly, the estimated increase in payroll taxes or reduction in benefits needed to maintain solvency is much greater than for Social Security.[25] The uncertainty regarding changes in Medicare going forward will have an especially large impact on prospective retirees, since they will be major consumers of health care services.

What's So Different about Decumulation?

The focus of financial planning for retirement is on the need for investors to accumulate enough wealth, through saving and investment decisions, during their working years to finance consumption throughout their retirement. In other words, investors need to maximize the value of their savings at age 65 for the level of risk that they are willing to take on. As workers retire, however, their objective turns into developing an optimal plan for asset decumulation—the spending down of their accumulated wealth. With the retirement of the baby boomers looming, demand will increase for advice and products that help investors understand, plan, and implement their preferred decumulation strategy. There are conceptual differences in optimal asset accumulation and decumulation, and innovation will be necessary to meet investors' changing needs.

Optimal Asset Accumulation

Theories of optimal asset accumulation, also known as optimal portfolio choice theories, date to Markowitz (1952). Investors are assumed to want an average

23. AXA Equitable Retirement Scope, January 2007 (www.axaonline.com/axaimages/AXA_Retirement_Scope_2007.pdf).

24. The 2007 Annual Report of the Boards of Trustees of Federal Hospital Insurance and Federal Supplementary Medical Insurance Trust Fund (www.treas.gov/offices/economic-policy/reports/medicare-report-2007.pdf).

25. Ibid. Estimates in the 2007 report call for an immediate 122 percent increase in taxes or 51 percent decrease in benefits.

return and to dislike risk. The efficient frontier and optimal portfolio allocation model illustrates that when a risky asset is available, all investors would optimally choose a portfolio of the riskless asset and one particular portfolio of risky assets (the tangency portfolio). Those ideas are the basis for much of modern investment advice—investors should diversify their portfolio and structure their investments according to their risk aversion. Putting the individual optimization problem into a market context led to the capital asset pricing model (CAPM) and the equilibrium result that the tangency portfolio must be the value-weighted market portfolio of risky assets.[26] The CAPM itself suggests another piece of advice commonly given by the Chicago School economists and John Bogle: invest in a passive index fund.

A voluminous academic and practitioner literature based on those ideas has evolved regarding how to evaluate mutual fund performance and develop strategies to beat the market. Strategies employ statistical tools like alpha, beta, style attribution, and measures of market timing, and they include empirical "regularities" regarding the performance of small-cap versus large-cap stocks, low versus high book-to-market stocks, the role of return momentum, and so forth. What is common in all the advice on strategy, however, is the objective—to improve average investment returns without increasing risk. In essence, investors need to know only their own willingness to trade risk for reward (more precisely, their risk aversion) in order to structure their investments, at least to a first-order approximation. The role of more advanced aspects of optimal portfolio choice (for example, additional risk factors such as inflation or macroeconomic risk) or the advantages of tax-efficient portfolio management are in a sense second-order concerns; certainly much less attention is focused on those topics by information intermediaries and retail investors as a whole.

There is one other major decision to be made in the wealth accumulation phase—the amount to invest. That is effectively the saving-versus-consumption decision that is standard in much of economics; it is similar to smaller decisions faced by individuals every day when they save for short-term goals like buying a new car or making a down payment on a house. Apart from the specifics of how the investment will be managed, individuals need to assess their own willingness to give up current consumption in order to save money to finance future consumption—in this case, after retirement. Formally, that decision is modeled as a function of an individual's personal discount rate on future consumption (that is, the rate at which he or she prefers current to future consumption), the horizon over which the consumption trade-off will occur, and the distribution of the

26. Sharpe (1964) and Lintner (1965).

uncertain return on the investment. In the context of saving for retirement, the horizon is often very long (forty years for a 25-year-old), the cost of saving in terms of forgone current consumption is immediately obvious, and, throughout much of their traditional saving years, individuals have the ability to increase savings if the returns on their investments do not meet expectations.

As retirement approaches, however, individuals' ability to increase their saving rate becomes less powerful. Research has found that one strategy for dealing with that fact is for investors to decrease the risk exposure of their investments as they age. Essentially, the approach of a retirement date has the same effect on an investor's portfolio as an increase in risk aversion; the solution is to reduce exposure to equities and high-risk investments and shift assets into bonds and other low-volatility or guaranteed assets.

The Optimal Decumulation Problem

The decision facing an individual on the brink of retirement is in a sense the opposite of the accumulation decision. In the accumulation phase, the investor works toward amassing a pool of assets; in the decumulation phase he or she must decide how to spread out the spending, or disbursement, of those assets. There are not many analogs to that decision in other areas of an individual's life. In some ways the decision is similar to setting a budget for clothing for the month and then deciding how to allocate the lump sum. In such decisions, the impact of any uncertainty (the risk of finding the perfect outfit later in the month, when the money's gone) is quite small; the next month will bring a new budget and new opportunities. Uncertainty and risk play a much larger role in the decision regarding decumulation strategies. Fundamentally that is because retirees have limited opportunities to add to their assets if a costly negative shock should occur. One option is for individuals to extend their working years or return to work, and indeed there is a trend in that direction. According to the Employee Benefits Research Institute, 48.9 percent of individuals in the 65–69 age group were working full time in 2005; in 1987, the figure was only 36.4 percent.[27]

A decumulation strategy commonly suggested by practitioners and advisers is to maintain a portfolio of invested assets and systematically withdraw a fraction of it each year. The time over which any withdrawal rate will provide income is a function of the uncertain future returns on the invested portfolio—which is itself a function of the allocation of assets to various classes (for example, equities and bonds)—and the prevailing rates of inflation in the future. Therefore, retirees face a significant degree of longevity risk—the risk that they will outlive their

27. Copeland (2007).

retirement assets—with a systematic withdrawal strategy. One oft-recommended example is the "4 percent rule," whereby 4 percent of a portfolio is withdrawn the first year and the dollar amount is then increased each year to keep pace with inflation. If one assumes a 10 percent average return on large-cap stocks, 6.5 percent on domestic bonds, and 4.75 percent on short-term "cash" and a 3 percent inflation rate, the 4 percent rule has a 90 percent probability of providing thirty years of retirement income when the underlying portfolio is weighted 60 percent, 30 percent, and 10 percent in stocks, bonds, and cash, respectively.[28]

Note that the systematic withdrawal strategy still exposes the retiree to risk—if the actual returns on the invested portfolio are lower or inflation is higher, there will be a significant probability of not meeting the income goal of 4 percent per year plus an inflation adjustment for the full thirty years. While there is a small chance (5 percent for women and 1.4 percent for men) that a retiree will live five more years, to 100 years of age, there is a much larger chance that the retiree will die prior to age 95 and leave positive assets.[29] If the retiree had no desire to leave a bequest, that outcome would result in underconsumption in the sense that the retiree could have sustained a higher withdrawal rate if he had known in advance how long he would live.

The academic research literature has focused on a very different strategy for decumulation. For a person without a bequest motive facing an uncertain lifetime, Yaari (1965) showed that it was optimal for the person to fully annuitize his or her wealth. The simplest form of annuitization involves entering into a contract, with payment up front, that entitles the bearer to regular payments for the remainder of his or her life. Upon the person's death, the issuer of the annuity has no further payment obligations.

Under full annuitization, that feature of a simple annuity implies that there will be no assets left to bequeath to heirs. For many retirees that may be undesirable. Partial annuitization "solves" the problem in the sense that the non-annuitized wealth can be bequeathed, and the size of the desired bequest will be a key factor in the decision regarding the fraction of wealth to be annuitized. For that reason, partial annuitization may be especially attractive to retirees with enough assets to generate an acceptable income and also leave a bequest.

Full annuitization of assets ensures a retiree against longevity risk—the income that they receive from the annuity is guaranteed for their lifetime. However, there is another risk that annuitization actually exacerbates, liquidity risk. If all of a

28. See T. Rowe Price retirement income calculator for a representative example of a Monte Carlo simulation with these assumptions (www3.troweprice.com/ric/RIC/).

29. Society of Actuaries, RP-2000 mortality tables (www.soa.org/research/files/pdf/rp00_mortality tables.pdf).

retiree's wealth is annuitized, there is no pool of assets to draw on when unexpected expenses arise. In contrast, a systematic withdrawal strategy preserves liquidity and allows a retiree to vary the withdrawal rate.

In the years since Yaari's original article, the theoretical research on the extent to which annuitization is an optimal strategy has expanded to include models such as variable payout annuities, annuities linked to stock market returns and inflation, dynamic strategies involving delayed annuitization, and more complicated annuity contracts with death benefits.[30] A recent study, based on a rich model of dynamic annuitization using variable payout annuities, finds that systematic withdrawals are "distinctly suboptimal, such that they [retirees] would have to be given up to 40 percent more initial wealth to leave them as well off as with variable payout annuities."[31] That general characterization of the optimality of some type of variable annuity strategy is supported by many other research studies and holds for retirees with and without a bequest motive.

When choosing the specifics of an optimal retirement income strategy, a retiree should evaluate several characteristics of his or her preferences and circumstances. How willing is he to trade liquidity risk for longevity risk? How willing is she to trade her own consumption in retirement for the consumption of her heirs after she is gone? How long does he expect to live and how much does he expect to have to spend on health care? Will her family act as a safety net if her assets run out or if she requires additional income in any given year? How risk averse is he—how much uncertainty is he willing to tolerate with respect to the value of his assets and his future consumption? Is she willing to continue working past her retirement age or to go back to work to supplement her investment or annuity income?

Innovation Going Forward

Twenty years ago most workers participated in a defined benefit pension plan which, in addition to Social Security, provided a base of guaranteed income during retirement. Today, on average, workers have very little expectation of receiving guaranteed income and must take on the task of managing their own retirement savings and financial planning. Those developments have so far been met with innovation in the area of advice, products, and industry structures to meet the needs of workers in the wealth accumulation years. Innovation is likely to continue but to focus on products and services geared toward young workers, who will con-

30. For an example of a fully dynamic model with variable annuities see Horneff and others (2007). For an example of real annuities and inflation hedging, see Brown, Mitchell, and Poterba (1999).
31. Horneff and others (2007), p. 4.

tinue to be a large market as they age. As the first of the baby boomers move into retirement, innovations also are likely to address the demands of investors in the decumulation phase. Some innovation already has been seen in anticipation of the rise in demand for retirement-related products.

As noted, the accumulation and decumulation decisions are quite different; that fact implies that mutual fund families will be motivated to change and expand the current menu of products and services to meet new demands. As with prior innovation in this market, activity can be expected from firms outside the industry as well as from mutual fund families. The insurance industry is the obvious competitor for managing the decumulation of retirees' assets. The central question for mutual fund families, then, is whether they will be able to maintain control of assets as current clients move from accumulating to decumulating their wealth.

Certainly the most direct path to maintaining control of assets while meeting investors' needs for retirement income is for mutual fund families to innovate in the area of systematic withdrawal plans. In effect, such plans just layer a withdrawal policy on top of a fund-of-funds mutual fund portfolio (either a constant lifestyle-type mix of stocks, bonds, and cash or a changing lifecyle-type allocation). Typically the choice of withdrawal rate, the management of withdrawals, and the choice of an underlying mutual fund portfolio has been left to investors themselves. Recently, however, Fidelity and Vanguard announced plans to launch new fund offerings that package a systematic schedule of monthly fund distributions (withdrawals) along with a risk-based mutual fund portfolio investment.[32]

Given the academic research advocating the use of partial annuitization, fund families might be expected to face stiff competition from insurance companies that provide annuity products. However, investors currently are not following the academic advice on optimal decumulation, and the market for individual annuities is quite small. It seems reasonable then to assume that insurance companies also will be motivated to innovate in order to increase investor demand for these products. The form that innovation will take depends, of course, on why investor demand is low right now. What is stopping investors from annuitizing? Recent research suggests that the most likely reasons are that families can act as self-insurance programs that substitute for annuitization (that is, spouses can pool their longevity risk) and that traditional annuity products lack liquidity.[33] Investor concern about lack of liquidity can be exacerbated by health status. Recent innovations in the annuity market include products for the "impaired" market—for

32. Daisy Maxey, "New Vanguard Funds Aim to Lure Retirees," *Wall Street Journal*, October 1, 2007, and David Hoffman, "Fidelity Debuts Retirement Products," *Investment News*, October 3, 2007.

33. Jeffrey Brown, "Life Annuities and Uncertain Lifetimes," *NBER Reporter*, Spring 2004, and studies cited therein.

example, those with chronic diseases such as multiple sclerosis or cancer. In addition, Lincoln National has launched a new variable annuity product with an enhancement to increase flexibility in timing income payments.

In a bid to reach baby boomers before retirement, when annuitization decisions typically are made, several insurers have begun marketing annuities to 401(k) plans.[34] While reported take-up has not been large (some fifty to sixty plan sponsors across four insurance providers) and challenges exist with regard to recordkeeping, there is reason to suspect that this trend or some version of it will continue. Complementing the push into the defined contribution market from annuity producers is the shift toward offering advice on decumulation strategies by firms supplying defined contribution plan participants with financial advice. Financial Engines Inc. is currently in a research phase while TIAA-CREF seeks to offer proprietary advice on decumulation to its participants.[35] Such advice can serve to educate investors on the benefits of annuitization and its place in a personalized decumulation plan. By decreasing decisionmaking and information gathering costs and increasing investors' understanding—and thus their comfort level—such efforts may increase the demand for annuities.

As mentioned, large mutual fund families are really better characterized as financial service providers. It is not surprising, therefore, that some have moved outside their core portfolio management business to offer clients annuity products as well. That, however, requires a fundamentally different business model and different risk management techniques. Annuities are primarily an insurance product, whose risk is managed by the insurer; in mutual fund management, the investment risk remains with the investor. Mutual fund families have confronted that issue through two industry structure innovations: one, the purchase or establishment of an insurance subsidiary; two, joint ventures, similar to subadvisory relationships, with insurance companies that provide annuity management. The mutual fund family, rather than using a supermarket structure, often brands the annuities (for example, Fidelity Growth and Guaranteed Income).

The decumulation decision seems to be much more idiosyncratic than the accumulation decision, involving more individual factors, such as family status and health issues. That implies that advice related to retirement income planning will likely need be more individualized. Each retiree might sit down with a financial adviser to build a customized plan, but the cost of providing such "face time" is high. Innovations in advice provision therefore are likely to evolve on the basis

34. Jenna Gottlieb, "Annuities Fan Fare Hitting a Sour Note," PIonline, June 25, 2007 (www.pionline.com). Examples include Hartford, MetLife, Genworth, and Prudential.

35. Jenna Gottlieb, "Advice Providers Go into Withdrawal," PIonline, September 3, 2007 (www.pionline.com).

of their scalability. Some financial advisers will be able to profit through the use of the packaged mutual fund products mentioned earlier; because much of the planning and withdrawal management function is built into those products, the adviser can more efficiently choose and present clients with a suitable strategy from a small menu of choices.

Computer modeling and automated decisionmaking tools are another avenue to cost-efficient provision of individualized planning. Several large mutual fund families already have added retirement income calculators and tools to their websites. The T. Rowe Price retirement income calculator, for example, uses Monte Carlo analysis to provide estimates of a sustainable retirement income based on investors' level of risk aversion, retirement horizon, marital status, assets, and income. But sophisticated analytics still require investors and retirees to devote time and effort to acquiring expertise and making decisions about the value of such calculations and how to use them in implementing a retirement strategy. Therefore, a natural complement to a slew of calculators is a thorough yet easily understandable program of basic retirement management advice that is designed to educate investors on what they can gain through good management of their assets and to illustrate how to put a plan together.

Again, new entrants from outside the traditional mutual fund and financial adviser industries are likely to play a role in providing that type of advice. The Pension Protection Act of 2006 allows employers to offer advice to defined contribution plan participants, a fact that is expected to spur innovation in advice provision through the employer-sponsored channel by firms like Financial Engines Inc. One tool that firms like these and other independent advice providers can use to enhance scalability is the dissemination of video lessons through the Internet. Indeed, videos related to annuity investment by Ben Stein and Thomas Scott already are on YouTube.

That raises the issue of how to leverage changing Internet technology to meet the specific demands of retirees. There is a significant literature on web design, and its findings are beginning to be applied in the mutual fund industry. Fidelity Investments operates the Fidelity Center for Applied Technology, which, among other projects, conducts research on designing websites to facilitate use by senior citizens. Among the challenges are how to design websites for individuals with visual, cognitive, or physical limitations (for example, arthritis) and those unfamiliar with web navigation. Among their interesting findings is that senior citizens tend to engage in "cautious clicking," whereby they hover over a link for a while before clicking on it. One explanation is that seniors may be wary of where the link might take them. Fidelity has proposed solutions, such as improving labels on links—for example, labeling a link "View Accounts" rather than just the generic "Accounts"—or adding pop-up descriptions to links to reassure users about what the link leads to. It seems safe to say that more individualized enhancements of web content and advice will be seen going forward.

As noted, although baby boomers represent large growth in the future population of retirees, the population of traditional savers (ages 40 to 60) will remain even higher. Mutual fund families are likely to find continuing innovation to serve this set of clients quite profitable. Given the importance of establishing client accounts, the first wave of innovation may target today's young workers (ages 25 to 40). Establishing client relationships with such potential investors early on could translate into long-term profitability for fund families. Some innovation in that direction already has appeared. Schwab and American Century, for example, have lowered minimum investments on certain fund products to appeal to young workers. American Century's initiative is called "My Whatever Plan" and includes target date funds out to 2050. Fund minimums typically exist to cover the fixed costs of fund administration and recordkeeping. To maintain profitability with lower minimums, several families restrict account information to web-only access or charge small incremental fees over time for additional services.

Web use is quite high, and social networking sites are quite popular among 25- to 40-year-olds. Again, innovations in investor education by third-party firms are beginning to appear on YouTube and MySpace. For example, FeelSmartAbout is a financial education start-up that uses animated videos on those sites to prompt interest in its other products, including a service to provide video lessons by e-mail. It is still unclear whether young workers will turn to independent financial advisers for help, feel satisfied with their ability to plan by using web tools and advice from fund companies, or do most of their planning and investing through employer-sponsored programs. Over time, all of those groups can be expected to experiment with serving young workers where they feel most comfortable—online and with their friends.

Conclusion

The old adage that "the only thing that stays the same is change" bears repeating, and the mutual fund industry is no exception to the rule. Over the past forty years the investing public has been the recipient of a vast array of innovations within the industry that have significantly increased wealth and welfare. The future promises more of the same as mutual fund families, financial advisers, information intermediaries, insurance companies, and new, as-yet-unnamed firms compete to satisfy the changing demands of U.S. investors.

The predictable shift of 80 million baby boomers from work to retirement provides some guidance in forecasting what changes are in store for the industry. The significant differences between asset accumulation and decumulation will spur innovation in mutual fund products, services, advice, and industry structure to meet new needs. In addition, continuing progress in the development of technology and the Internet will ensure that innovation continues in the provision of traditional mutual fund portfolio management services.

References

Bodie, Zvi, Robert C. Merton, and William F. Samuelson. 1992. "Labor Supply Flexibility and Portfolio Choice in a Lifecycle Model." *Journal of Economic Dynamics and Control* 16 (3–4): 427–49.

Brown, Jeffrey R., Olivia Mitchell, and James M.. Poterba. 1999. "The Role of Real Annuities and Indexed Bonds in an Individual Retirement Program." Working Paper 7005. Cambridge, Mass.: National Bureau of Economic Research.

Copeland, Craig. 2007. "Employment Status of Workers Ages 55 and Older," *EBRI Notes* 28 (8) (Employee Benefits Research Institute).

Del Guercio, Diane, Jonathan Reuter, and Paula A. Tkac. 2007. "Who Picks Stocks for the Competition: The Economics of Mutual Fund Subadvisory Contracts." Working paper. University of Oregon, Department of Finance.

Del Guercio, Diane, and Paula A. Tkac. Forthcoming. "Star Power: The Effect of Morningstar Ratings on Mutual Fund Flows." *Journal of Financial and Quantitative Analysis*.

Frame, Scott W., and Lawrence J. White. 2004. "Empirical Studies of Financial Innovation: Lots of Talk, Little Action?" *Journal of Economic Literature* 42 (1): 116–44.

Gastineau, Gary L. 2002. *The Exchange Traded Funds Manual*. New York: John Wiley and Sons.

Horneff, Wolfram J., and others. 2007. "Money in Motion: Dynamic Portfolio Choice in Retirement." Working Paper 12942. Cambridge, Mass.: National Bureau of Economic Research.

Lintner, John. 1965. "The Valuation of Risk Assets and the Selection of Risky Investments in Stock Portfolios and Capital Budgets." *Review of Economics and Statistics* 47 (1): 13–37.

Markowitz, Harry. 1952. "Portfolio Selection." *Journal of Finance* 7 (1): 77–91.

Sharpe, William F. 1964. "Capital Asset Prices: A Theory of Market Equilibrium under Conditions of Risk." *Journal of Finance* 19 (3): 425–42.

Simon, Curtis, and Robert Tamura. 2007. "Fertility Decline and Baby Boom." Working paper. Clemson University, Walker Department of Economics.

Tufano, Peter. 2003. "Financial Innovation." In *Handbook of the Economics of Finance*, vol.1A, edited by George M. Constantinides, Milt Harris, and René M. Stulz. Amsterdam: Elsevier B.V.

Yaari, Menahem E. 1965. "Uncertain Lifetime, Life Insurance, and the Theory of the Consumer." *Review of Economic Studies* 32 (2): 137–50.

KOICHI IWAI 2

The Future of Japan's
Mutual Fund Industry

C OMPARED WITH THE markets in other countries, Japan's market for mutual
funds (which normally take the form of investment trusts) is small relative
to the size of the national economy (figure 2-1). The fraction of household financial assets represented by mutual funds is increasing in both the United States and
Germany, where it is now more than 10 percent, while it has been only about 2
to 4 percent in Japan. That is a sizable difference (figure 2-2).

Factors in Recent Growth in Japan's Mutual Fund Industry

Although small relative to markets in other countries, Japan's investment trust
market began growing around 2003 (figure 2-3), probably owing to changes in
market conditions, distribution channels, product innovation, and demographics.

Market Conditions

I begin by confirming the relationship between investment returns and the inflow
of funds into investment trusts. Figure 2-4 shows the equity-deposit spread
(return on equities minus the savings deposit interest rate) over time.[1] As shown

---

1. Nakagawa and Katagiri (1999), which presents a detailed analysis of risk asset investment behavior
in Japan's household sector, uses the equity-deposit spread as a proxy variable for the return on risk assets.
I follow that paper and run an empirical analysis using the equity-deposit spread as a proxy for mutual fund
returns.

Figure 2-1. *Mutual Fund Net Assets as Percentage of Nominal GDP*[a]

Percent

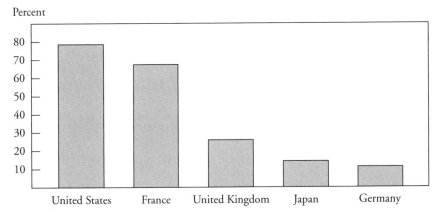

Sources: Author's calculations based on *Investment Company Fact Book 2007* (Investment Company Institute), National Economic Accounts (U.S. Department of Commerce), Annual National Accounts (French National Institute of Statistics and Economic Studies), United Kingdom National Accounts (Office for National Statistics), National Accounts (Deutsche Bundesbank), Long-Term Time-Series Data (Investment Trusts Association, Japan), and Quarterly Estimates of GDP (Cabinet Office, Japan).

a. Figure for Japan is fund assets in March 2007 as percentage of 2006 nominal GDP. U.S. data are as of year-end 2006. France, U.K., and Germany data are as of year-end 2005.

Figure 2-2. *Mutual Funds as Percentage of Household Financial Assets*[a]

Percent

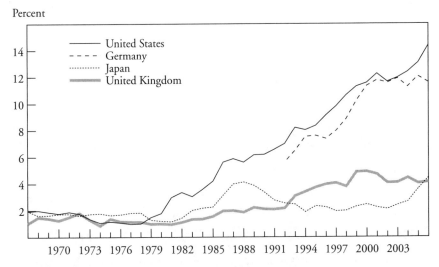

Sources: Author's calculations based on Flow of Funds Accounts (Federal Reserve Bank), Financial Accounts (Deutsche Bundesbank), National Statistics (Bank of England), and Flow of Funds (Bank of Japan).

a. Figures for Japan are as of fiscal year end; all others are as of calendar year end.

Figure 2-3. *Net Assets of Investment Trusts in Japan*

Yen (trillions)

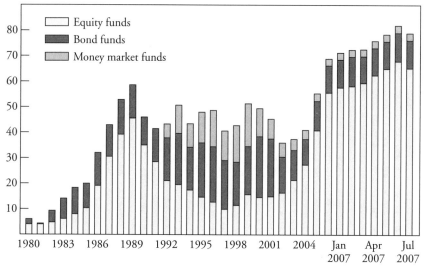

Source: Long-Term Time-Series Data (Investment Trusts Association, Japan).

in figure 2-3, there was a large influx of funds into equity investment trusts in the late 1980s and again in the mid 2000s, periods during which total assets held in investment trusts grew and the equity-deposit spread remained high for several years. In the 1990s, however, there was an exodus of funds from equity investment trusts, and the equity-deposit spread remained largely negative during that period.[2] The inflow of funds into investment trusts is strongly influenced by prevailing share price and interest rate trends.

I attempt here to examine the quantitative impact that such market trends have on that inflow. As explained later, however, the popularity in Japan of funds that invest in foreign currency–denominated assets makes it essential to include the impact of currency rate fluctuations as a market factor (figure 2-5). I therefore estimate a vector autoregression (VAR) model with three variables: the equity-deposit spread, the month-on-month change in the nominal effective exchange rate, and the net inflow of funds into equity investment trusts.[3] To evaluate the impact of the yen's depreciation since 2003, I use two estimation periods. The

2. Funds flowed into money market funds and bond investment trusts in the late 1990s, with one likely reason being the relatively high rates of interest paid at the time.

3. After running the Phillips-Perron (PP) test on each variable, I found that the nominal effective exchange rate was a first-difference stationary process—I (1) process—and that the rest were level stationary

Figure 2-4. Equity Return versus Deposit Interest Rate

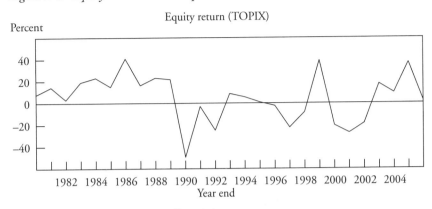

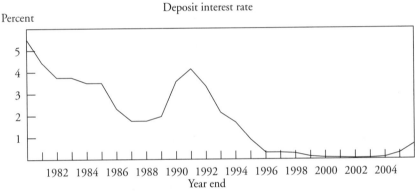

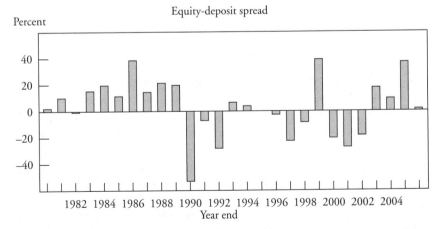

Source: Author's calculations based on International Financial Statistics (Bank for International Settlements) and TOPIX (Tokyo Stock Exchange).

Figure 2-5. *Net Inflow of Funds into Open-Ended Equity Investment Trusts versus Share Price and Forex Trends*[a]

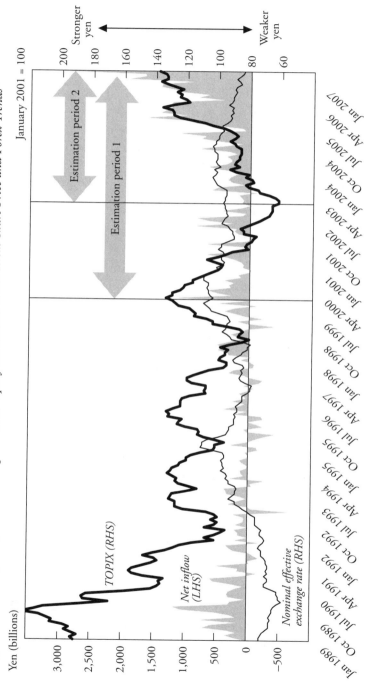

Source: Author's calculations based on TOPIX (Tokyo Stock Exchange), Effective Exchange Rates (Bank of Japan), and Long-Term Time-Series Data (Investment Trusts Association, Japan).

a. Nominal effective exchange rate and TOPIX are on a scale with January 2000 = 100. LHS = left-hand side; RHS = right-hand side.

first estimation period is from February 2000 to April 2007, corresponding to the period after the information technology bubble burst, and the second estimation period is from April 2003 until April 2007, which was a period of yen depreciation and stock market strength.

Figure 2-6 shows the extent to which the net investment trust inflow reacts to an increase in the equity-deposit spread and a weakening of the yen. One sees first that, for both estimation periods, investment trust inflow increases when the equity-deposit spread increases and the yen weakens. Second, we see that during the period of yen depreciation and share price appreciation that began in 2003 (the second estimation period), the inflow was more sensitive to yen weakness than it was to the equity-deposit spread.

Figure 2-7 shows the explanatory power of the three variables in regard to the variance of the net funds inflow. First, the explanatory power of the combined effects of the equity-deposit spread and nominal exchange rates was about 40 percent after four months. In other words, about 40 percent of the short-term change in funds inflow was caused by market fluctuations.[4] Second, the exchange rate had a greater impact in the second estimation period than it did in the first. Once the yen entered its depreciation phase, the impact of exchange rate changes on the investment trust inflow became stronger.

Regardless, that suggests the possibility that as the investment trust industry has grown over the past few years, a rising stock market and weakening yen have stimulated an inflow of funds into investment trusts. Conversely, there is the possibility that a falling stock market and strengthening yen would serve to suppress the inflow of funds.

Distribution Channels

Distribution channels also are an important factor affecting the size of the market. I think that two regulatory changes affecting distribution channels have played an especially important role in the Japanese market's recent growth. The first was the regulatory change that allowed both banks and the post office to handle the sale of

---

processes—I (0) processes—at a significance level of 5 percent. The VAR lag order was based on the Akaike information criterion (AIC).

4. My results lead to an opinion that differs from that of the existing literature analyzing the relationship between market changes and the inflow of funds into U.S. mutual funds. For example, Remolona, Keiman, and Gruenstein (1997) found that market changes had almost no impact on mutual fund inflows, while Warther (1995) found that a rising market led to fund outflows. Nevertheless, because the processing and estimation methods used on the net flow data presented in this chapter differ from the methods used in those studies, it is impossible to strictly compare the results.

Figure 2-6. *Impulse Response Function of Net Inflows into Equity Investment Trusts*[a]

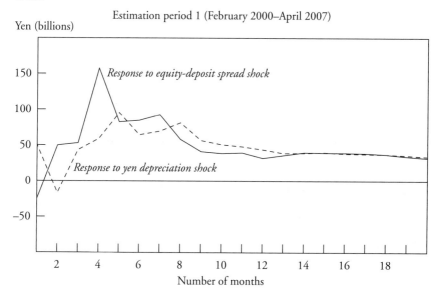

Estimation period 1 (February 2000–April 2007)

Yen (billions)

Response to equity-deposit spread shock

Response to yen depreciation shock

Number of months

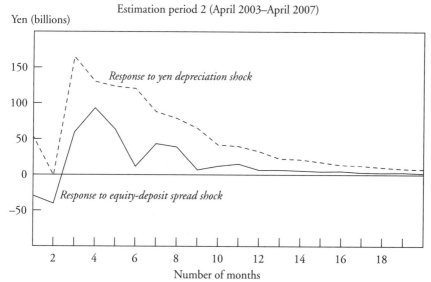

Estimation period 2 (April 2003–April 2007)

Yen (billions)

Response to yen depreciation shock

Response to equity-deposit spread shock

Number of months

Source: Author's calculations.

a. I used a VAR model with three variables: the equity-deposit spread, the month-on-month change in the nominal effective exchange rate, and the net inflow of funds.

Figure 2-7. *Variance Decomposition Analysis of Net Inflows into Equity Investment Trusts*[a]

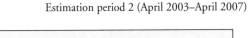

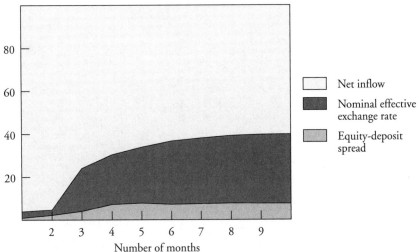

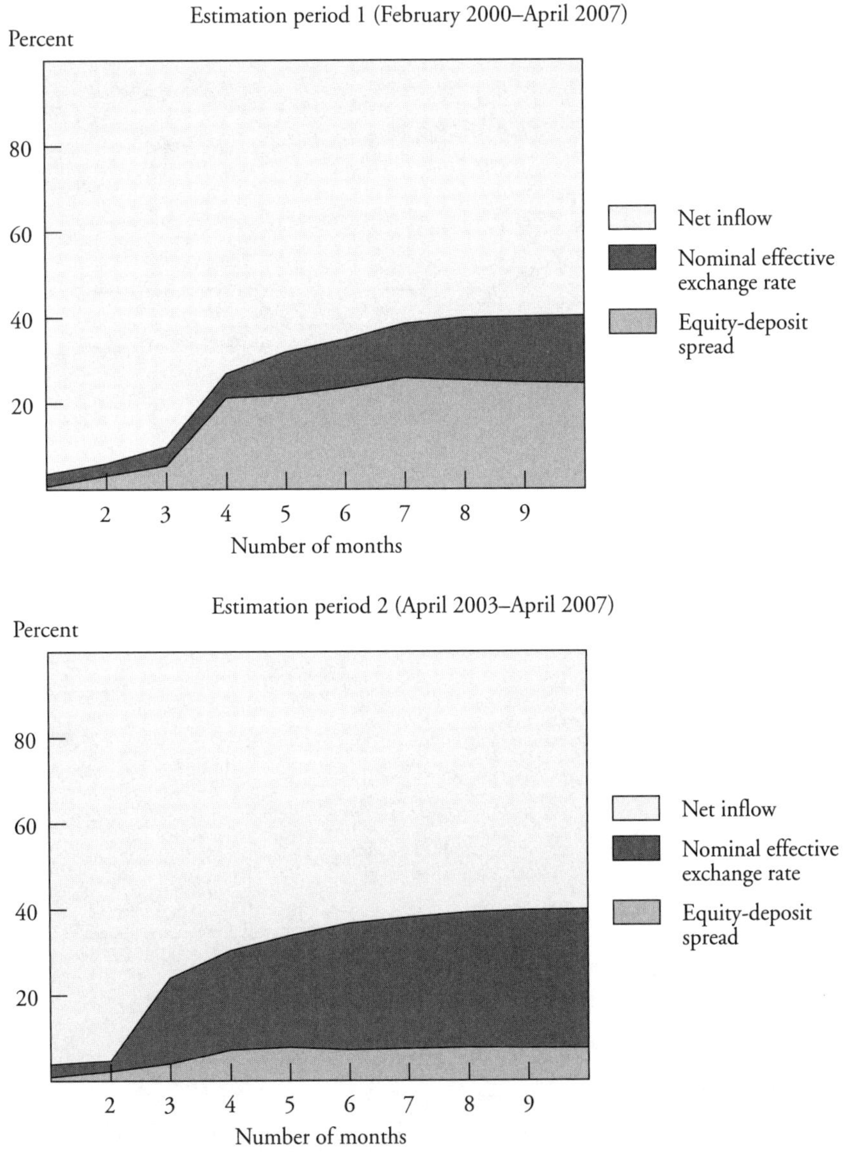

Source: Author's calculations.

a. I used a VAR model with three variables: the equity-deposit spread, the month-on-month change in the nominal effective exchange rate, and the net inflow of funds.

Figure 2-8. *Equity Investment Trusts (Net Assets) by Distribution Channel*[a]

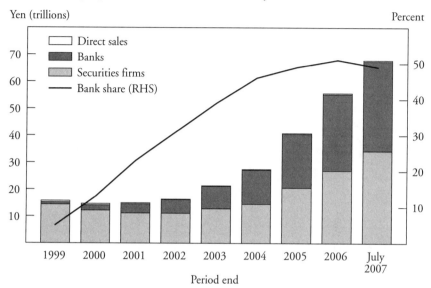

Yen (trillions)

Percent

Period end

Source: Author's calculations based on Total Net Assets of Investment Trusts of Contractual Type by Distribution Channel (Investment Trusts Association, Japan).
a. "Banks" includes sales by Japan Post since 2005. RHS = right-hand side.

investment trusts. There has been a steady expansion of distribution channels following the lifting of the restriction on retail sales of investment trusts by banks in December 1998 and the launching of investment trust sales by the post office in 2005.[5] Figure 2-8 shows the total net assets within investment trusts by distribution channel.[6] The quantity of assets brought in through banks has grown substantially since they began retail sales in 1998.

The second regulatory change was the introduction of defined contribution pension plans. The number of people participating in defined contribution plans has steadily increased since their introduction in 2001 (figure 2-9). According to the Ministry of Health, Labor, and Welfare, investment trusts accounted for about 38 percent of all assets invested with defined contribution plans at the end

5. Prior to that, one step taken to deregulate sales was a change made in December 1997 that allowed fund managers to rent space within bank branches and sell their funds there.
6. The value of investment trusts sold over the Internet in Japan is quite small at this point, only ¥412.3 billion in FY2005 and ¥531.6 billion in FY2006 (based on asset value), according to the Japan Security Dealers Association (JSDA).

Figure 2-9. *Number of Participants in Defined Contribution Pension Plans*[a]

Participants   Participants

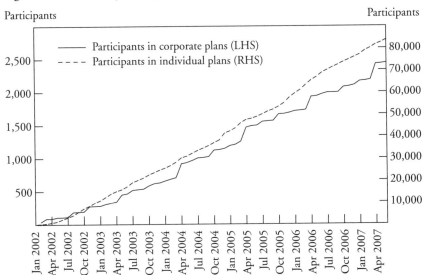

Source: 401k Jiji Press (Jiji Press Ltd) [http://401k.jiji.com/401k/401kTop.html].
a. LHS = left-hand side; RHS = right-hand side.

of FY2006.[7] There is also empirical research showing a relationship in other countries between the introduction of defined contribution plans and growth in the mutual fund market.[8]

Product Innovation

Product innovation is another factor in market growth. Figure 2-10, which plots the number of equity investment trust products against total net assets, shows a major change in the relationship between the two around 2004. Since 2004, total net assets have grown considerably faster than the number of products offered. As shown in figure 2-11, growth of total net assets was largely in balanced funds (paying monthly dividends) and funds of funds. Another notable characteristic of this period has been the rising proportion of foreign currency–denominated assets (figure 2-12). Furthermore, superfunds larger than ¥1 trillion have emerged, which are mostly of those two types. While six funds exceeded ¥1 trillion at the end of December 2006, five among them belonged to the two categories.

7. In contrast, products with guaranteed principal account for roughly 60 percent.
8. Khorana, Servaes, and Tufano (2005).

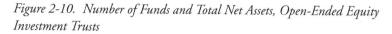

Figure 2-10. Number of Funds and Total Net Assets, Open-Ended Equity Investment Trusts

Yen (billions)

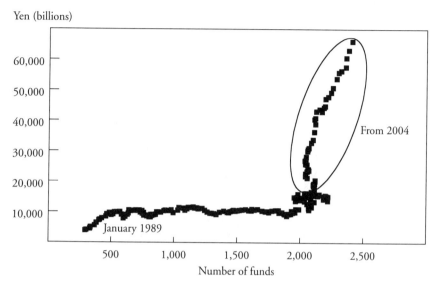

Source: Author's calculations based on Long-Term Time-Series Data (Investment Trusts Association, Japan).

Balanced funds and funds of funds may predominate because they have met investor needs in two respects. First, they pay monthly dividends. Figure 2-13 shows the results of a survey on reasons for holding investment trusts. As explained later, the main buyers of investment trusts are those 40 years of age and older. These age cohorts are interested not only in price appreciation and safety, but also in the frequency and size of dividends. During the last decade of super-low interest rates, the investment trusts that suited the needs of these investors have apparently been those that invest in overseas bonds with the potential for high yields and monthly-dividend investment trusts, which offer a regular stream of income.

The second way that these funds meet investor needs is the high degree of safety that they offer. Table 2-1 compares the risk (standard deviation) of investment returns by type of fund. In 2006 balanced funds and funds of funds had relatively low risk (the average value shown in the table), probably a reflection of the benefits of diversifying into multiple asset classes. Furthermore, the riskiness of balanced funds has been declining since 2001.

Recent growth in the investment trust market, then, probably can be attributed to the offering of monthly dividends as demanded by investors and to the

Figure 2-11. *Total Net Assets by Fund Type, Open-Ended Equity Investment Trusts*

Yen (trillions)

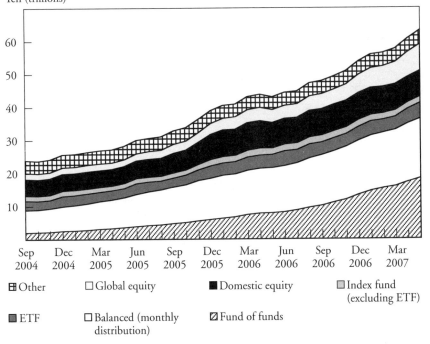

Source: "Report on Investment Trusts" (Investment Trusts Association, Japan).

fact that as a result of the decline in the investment risk of balance funds, the risk-return characteristics of investment trusts now more closely match the risk tolerance of investors.

Demographics

As suggested by the popularity of investment trusts that pay monthly dividends, there is a possibility that the aging of Japan's population also is fueling growth in the investment trust market. Figure 2-14, which compares the percentage of total savings invested in equities and equity investment trusts (risk assets) across age cohorts, makes clear that allocations to risk assets rise with age and that the trend became more pronounced in 2006.[9] Figure 2-15 shows the percentage of each age

9. For example, there was a large increase in allocation between 2000 and 2006 for the 60–69 and 70-and-older age cohorts.

Figure 2-12. *Distribution of Net Assets of Investment Trusts*

Yen (trillions)

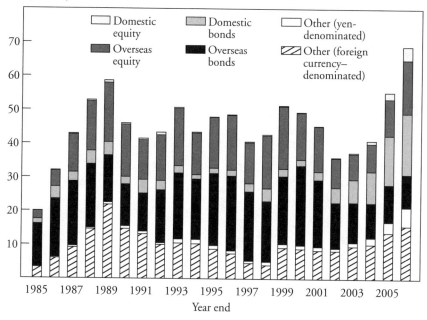

Source: "Report on Investment Trusts" (Investment Trusts Association, Japan).

cohort with ownership in investment trusts, indicating that the number of individuals in each age cohort who own investment trusts rises with age. One conceivable reason for the concentration of investment trust ownership in the older age cohorts is the change in the composition of household financial assets that occurs around the time of retirement. In Japan, it is common to use retirement payouts to pay off housing loans and other debt, and a household's net financial assets tend to increase after retirement. Households that experience an increase in net financial assets appear to be able to raise their allocations to investment trusts and other risk assets.

Recent growth in investment trusts, then, probably can be attributed to an increase in such investments by households whose members are 60 years of age and older and retired. Furthermore, given that the population age 60 and older will continue growing for the time being, demographics are expected to continue fueling growth in the investment trust industry. With that in mind, I explore quantitatively the extent to which demographic changes have brought growth in investment trusts.

Figure 2-13. *Deciding Factors in Investment Trust Purchases, November 2006*

Percent

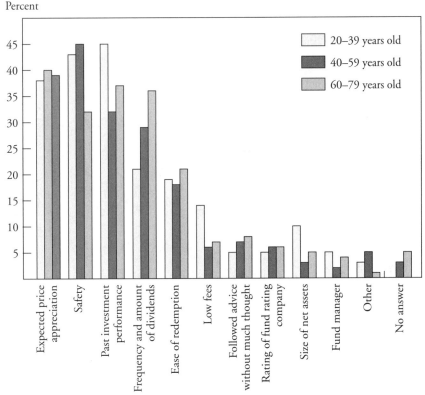

Source: "Toushi-shintaku ni kansuru ankeito chousa houkoku-sho"[Survey on Mutual Funds] (Investment Trusts Association, Japan).

My examination is based on a cohort analysis. Figure 2-16 shows the results, using the percent allocation to equity investment trusts (equity investment trusts divided by total savings) by age cohort as the dependent variable. One can draw several conclusions from the analysis. First, the percentage of savings invested in investment trusts rises with age. That is, there clearly is an increase in allocations to investment trusts as people get older.[10] Second, younger generations born in 1971 and later tend to allocate a greater share of their savings to investment trusts

10. Figure 2-14 shows the same relationship. Nevertheless, the upward sloping relationship in the figure represents a mixture of the age effect, the cohort effect, and the time effect, and thus it is not a straightforward assessment of the change in investment allocation that accompanies aging. In contrast, the age

Table 2-1. *Distribution of Investment Risk*[a]

Fund	Number of funds	Average	Minimum	Maximum	Standard deviation
December 2001					
Index fund	64	18.7	16.6	22.5	1.1
Balanced	158	7.8	0.1	28.1	4.7
Fund of funds	n.a.	n.a.	n.a.	n.a.	n.a.
Industry-specific index fund	27	25.0	16.5	38.0	7.0
Global equity	107	26.2	5.8	128.3	14.8
Domestic equity	188	28.0	10.7	71.5	12.2
June 2004					
Index fund	68	18.1	16.0	25.6	1.6
Balanced	213	6.2	0.0	14.2	3.4
Fund of funds	9	8.5	3.3	19.8	5.1
Industry-specific index fund	23	21.3	12.5	31.6	4.1
Global equity	112	22.0	6.7	75.7	8.9
Domestic equity	302	20.6	8.5	60.9	6.3
December 2006					
Index fund	84	16.2	13.0	18.6	0.8
Balanced	342	5.7	0.3	11.5	2.6
Fund of funds	65	7.3	0.6	20.5	5.5
Industry-specific index fund	22	20.9	10.8	32.5	5.1
Global equity	148	16.0	4.4	51.6	6.8
Domestic equity	328	19.2	1.9	50.9	6.7

Source: Author's calculations based on Principia (Morningstar).

a. Standard deviation of return over past three years; covers open-ended equity investment trusts with net assets of at least 1 billion yen.

than other generations. I believe that that reflects a lower resistance to newer financial products such as investment trusts among successively younger generations. Third, the parameter for the time effect shows an increase in the year 1990, probably because that year coincided with the bubble era.

Using the estimation results from my cohort analysis to predict the future path of investment trusts, I estimate that investment trust assets will be 45 percent higher in 2010 than in 2000 and that they will continue to grow in future years

effect in my cohort analysis simply shows the change in investment allocations that accompanies aging, although it includes estimation errors.

Figure 2-14. *Allocation to Risk Assets by Age Cohort*[a]

Percent

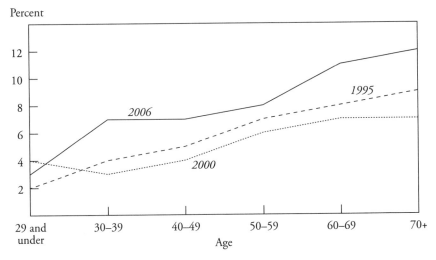

Source: Author's calculations based on the Family Income and Expenditure Survey (Ministry of Internal Affairs and Communications, Japan) and the Family Savings Survey (Statistics Bureau, Ministry of Internal Affairs and Communications).

a. Investments in equities and equity funds as a percentage of savings. Figures from 2006 are based on the Family Income and Expenditure Survey; figures from 2000 and 1995 are based on the Family Savings Survey.

(figure 2-17). That growth should be attributable mostly to age effects. Specifically, the age effect for equity investment trusts increased with age. Because the number of seniors in Japan is growing, investment in equity investment trusts also is growing. Furthermore, because these demographic changes will continue for the time being, demographics should continue to support the investment trust market.

Challenges for Further Advances

As the four factors outlined above suggest, recent growth in the investment trust market has been driven by both cyclical and structural factors. My analysis does not, however, provide clear evidence as to whether the cyclical factors or the structural factors have had the stronger impact. If the stock market continues to weaken and the yen continues to strengthen, there is a possibility that the rate of growth in investment trusts will slow from the pace observed since 2003. Signs of slowing already were evident in July 2007, when investment trust net assets actually declined in month-on-month terms. The sustainability of recent growth may be largely dependent on whether the measures outlined below are implemented.

Figure 2-15. *Ownership of Investment Trusts, FY2006*[a]

Percent

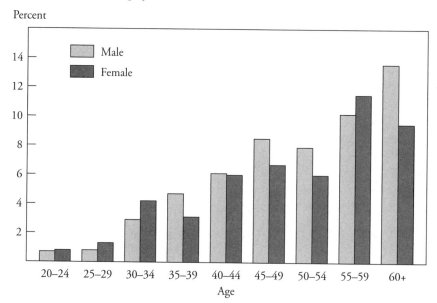

Source: "Heisei 18nendo shouken toushi ni kansuru zenkoku chousa" [FY2006 Nationwide Survey on Individual Securities Investment] (Japan Securities Dealers Association and Institute for Securities Education and Public Relations).

a. Figure shows the percentage of each age cohort that owns investment trusts.

Reform of Defined Contribution Pension Plans

When considering that growth in participation in 401(k) and IRA plans has been one factor behind the growth of the U.S. mutual fund industry since the 1980s, it seems likely that growth in the investor base can be achieved through the use of defined contribution pension plans, which have just recently gained momentum in Japan. Nevertheless, the rules governing Japan's plans are inferior to those in the United States for the purpose of expanding the investor base. First, there is a big difference in plan eligibility rules between Japan's individual defined contribution pensions and U.S. IRAs. Government workers and housewives are eligible for IRAs in the United States, but they are not allowed to enroll in Japan's individual defined contribution pensions. Second, there are big differences in the contribution amounts and contribution methods allowed for corporate defined contribution pensions. In addition to the maximum contribution being lower in Japan, there also are differences in contribution amounts depending on whether the individual is also enrolled in a defined benefit plan. Last, both company and employees are able to

54 KOICHI IWAI

Figure 2-16. *Cohort Analysis, Equity Investment Trusts/Savings*[a]

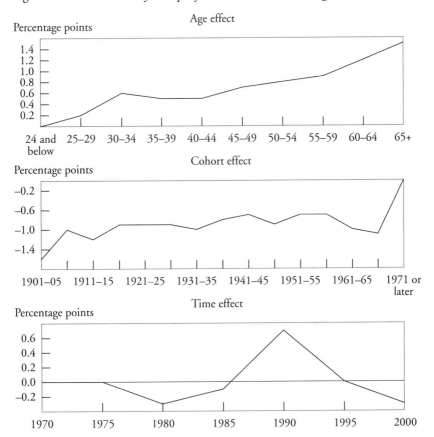

Source: Author's calculations based on the Family Income and Expenditure Survey (Ministry of Internal Affairs and Communications, Japan) and the Family Savings Survey (Statistics Bureau, Ministry of Internal Affairs and Communications).

a. Estimation model is as follows:

$$x_{it} = \beta_0 + \beta_i + \beta_t + \beta_c + \epsilon_{it},$$

where

X_{it}: Share of savings invested in equity investment trusts for age cohort i at time t.

β_i : Constant

β_i : Age effect

β_i : Time effect

β_i : Cohort effect

ϵ_{it} : Error term

Estimation period is 1970 to 2000 in five-year increments.

Estimation results: Adjusted R_2 = 0.41, F value - 2.73, P value = 0.001.

Figure 2-17. *Forecast for Japan's Investment Trust Market*[a]

Percentage points

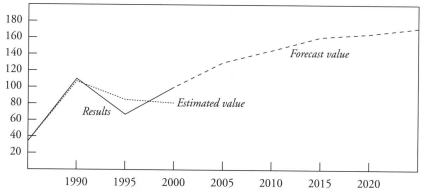

Source: Author's calculations based on the Family Income and Expenditure Survey (Ministry of Internal Affairs and Communications, Japan), the Family Savings Survey (Statistics Bureau, Ministry of Internal Affairs and Communications), and "Population Projections for Japan" (National Institute of Population and Social Security Research).

a. Forecasts are based on the following equation:

Forecast value for future time t = (savings per household in 2000) ×
(growth rate in savings per household) ×
(investment trusts as a percentage of savings for
each household at time t by age cohort) ×
(forecast number of households at time t by age cohort).

Forecasts are based on the following:

The growth rate in savings per household was assumed to be the same as in 2000.

For investment trusts as a percentage of savings for each household at time t by age cohort, estimation results in the cohort analysis were used; for 2000, actual figures were used.

For forecast number of households at time t by age cohort, estimates from the National Institute of Population and Social Security Research were used.

The percentage of households in each age cohort with ownership in investment trusts was assumed to remain the same in future years as in 2000.

The cohort effect for generations not yet born was assumed to be the same as for cohorts born in 1971 or later.

The time effect in the future was assumed to be the average of the time effects from 1985 to 2000.

contribute to a 401(k) plan in the United States, but employee contributions are not allowed in Japan. There have been calls from the business community to allow employee contributions, but at present the rules do not allow them.[11]

For investment trusts to gain a more solid foothold within defined contribution plans, remaining issues related to the handling of default products must be

11. A study group under the FSA's Financial System Council argues for the need to introduce a system of employee contributions (www.fsa.go.jp/singi/singi_kinyu/s_group/siryou/20070313.html). In addition,

resolved. Current regulations do not include any specific rules on the selection of default products, and it seems likely that the default products for nearly all defined contribution plans are products with guaranteed principal (time deposits).[12] According to a recent report, Pension Fund Association (2007), only 33.5 percent of the companies that offer defined contribution plans provide ongoing education for plan participants, who typically do not revise their portfolios after the initial investment selection.[13] It appears that in Japan, a time deposit is automatically selected as the default investment upon enrollment. In most cases there is no effort to revise asset allocations to keep in step with the participant's life cycle; the funds are just left parked in time deposits. Because of that, continuing education on defined contribution plans probably needs to be more readily available; in addition, after better understanding of participant behavior is gained, rules could be designed to ensure more suitable asset allocations.

Promoting Competition

Maintaining a sound competitive environment is not only critical for investors but also essential for the development of the industry overall. A competitive environment must be ensured for both the development and the sale of products. Whether there are conditions within Japan's investment trust industry that may restrict competition has been the subject of some debate.

DOMINATION OF INDUSTRY STRUCTURE BY THE MAJOR FINANCIAL GROUPS. Some observers have argued that there has been suppression of competition even in the U.S. mutual fund industry, which is thought to be more competitive than that of Japan. Specifically, Wallison and Litan (2007) argues that allowing boards of directors to decide on the commissions paid to related parties is a barrier to competition in setting commissions. It is impossible to apply arguments made with respect to the U.S. industry, in which most mutual funds are structured as corporations, directly to the industry in Japan, where investment trusts are structured primarily as contracts, but there is a possibility that Japan's industry structure suppresses competition.

---

in a recent survey of corporations that offer defined contribution plans, 65 percent of the companies that responded said that they would like to see the rules changed to allow for employee contributions; see NPO 401k Educational Society and Fidelity Investments Japan Limited (2007).

12. Contrast that with the situation in the United States, where the Pension Protection Act enacted in August 2006 holds that default investments that meet certain requirements (including lifecycle funds and balanced funds) can be treated as if there were investment instructions from the plan participant, effectively allowing mutual funds as default products.

13. In the United States, advances have been made in facilitating the creation of programs that are effective in raising 401(k) participation rates, based on studies of the behavior of 401(k) plan participants from a behavioral economics perspective; see Thaler and Benartzi (2004).

The most notable characteristic of Japan's investment trust industry is the dominant market share of asset management firms affiliated with major financial groups. In Japan, the top five companies control more than 60 percent of the market, and the top ten companies control close to 80 percent, making Japan's market considerably more concentrated than that of the United States. Table 2-2 shows the market share of asset management companies by the industry segment of their major shareholder. Independent asset management firms and foreign-capitalized asset management firms have low market shares, while asset management firms affiliated with securities houses or banks have high market shares. As a consequence of recent financial restructuring, it is not unusual for the major financial groups, especially large banks, to have a stake in several asset management firms. Certain asset investment management firms affiliated with the major financial groups thus dominate the upper rungs of Japan's investment industry, while the presence of the foreign-capitalized and independent firms is fairly small.

The major financial groups also have a substantial presence as distribution channels for investment trusts. One reason is the extensive sales networks owned by the leading financial groups; another is that the leading financial groups use their equity positions in the regional banks to forge close partnerships with those banks, in effect treating them as members of their group.[14] In Japan, both the formation and sale of investment trusts are concentrated in the major financial groups, resulting in less separation between the two functions than exists in the United States.

PREFERENTIAL TREATMENT FOR FUNDS FROM WITHIN THE GROUP. There is concern over the possibility that the lack of separation of functions suppresses competition between providers. Specifically, there is a possibility that major financial groups with their own asset management firms favor funds from those firms, regardless of commissions or performance. When the sales company selects an investment trust solely because it is managed by an affiliate, it inevitably limits investor choice.

I empirically examine how widespread the practice is of giving priority to investment trusts managed within the group by estimating the following logit model (estimation results are shown in table 2-3):

$$P \text{ (sales company } i \text{ handles fund } j) = F_L \text{ (group variable, control variables),}$$

where F_L is the cumulative logistic distribution function.

The dependent variable is 1 if the sales company handles the fund (includes it in its retail lineup) and 0 if it does not. The group variable is the percent stake

14. There also are cases in which the major financial group sends an employee to the regional bank to serve as a member of the bank's board of directors.

Table 2-2. *Market Share by Industry Segment, June 2007*
Yen (trillions)

Affiliate	Number	Total		Equity funds		Bond funds		Money market funds	
		Net assets	Market share (percent)	Net assets	Market share (percent)	Neet assets	Market share (percent)	Net assets	Market share (percent)
Domestic securities affiliates	4	40.9	50	29.3	43	9.3	83	2.3	78
Domestic bank affiliates	11	24.2	30	22.1	32	1.7	15	0.5	17
Domestic insurer affiliates	7	2.2	3	2.1	3	0.0	0	0.0	2
Domestic independents	17	1.3	2	1.2	2	0.1	1	0.1	2
Foreign capitalized affiliates	32	13.3	16	13.2	19	0.1	1	0.0	1
Total	71	82.0	100	67.9	100	11.2	100	2.9	100

Source: Author's calculations based on "Net Assets by Each Management Company" (Investment Trusts Association, Japan).

Table 2-3. *Estimation Results for Logit Model*[a]

Explanatory variable		Large banks (10 firms)		Regional banks (111 firms)		Securities firms (18 firms)	
		Coefficient	P value	Coefficient	P value	Coefficient	P value
Group variable	x 1	0.039	0.000	0.026	0.00	0.044	0.000
	x 2	0.017	0.000	0.333	0.00	0.055	0.000
	x 3			-0.335	0.35	0.382	0.000
	x 4			0.039	0.00		
Sales company's total commissions	x 5	-0.583	0.000	-0.097	0.05	0.199	0.014
Trust fees (trust company's portion)	x 6	14.885	0.000	3.854	0.05	-3.846	0.104
Trust fees (asset management firm's portion)	x 7	-0.797	0.172	-0.978	0.00	0.589	0.150
Net assets under management	x 8	0.139	0.004	0.410	0.00	0.196	0.000
Market share within the same Morningstar category	x 9	12.537	0.000	6.408	0.00	4.330	0.001
Number of stars from Morningstar	x 10	0.139	0.087	-0.158	0.00	0.135	0.003
Sharp ratio (1 year)	x 11	0.116	0.302	-0.155	0.01	0.208	0.025
Sharp ratio (3 year)	x 12	-0.290	0.066	0.454	0.00	-0.775	0.000
Number of years since inception	x 13	-0.055	0.073	0.137	0.00	0.276	0.000
Constant term	x 14	-4.498	0.000	-7.844	0.00	-7.071	0.000
Observations		5,370		59,607		10,178	
Pseudo R^2		0.234		0.113		0.235	

Source: Author's calculation.

a. Samples include only balanced funds and fund of funds defined by the Investment Trusts Association, Japan. Data for mutual funds are as of December 2006; group variables are calculated using information at March 2006.

in the sales company that is owned by the financial group to which the asset management firm belongs. The larger the group variable, the deeper the capital ties between the sales company and the asset management firm's affiliated financial group. When an asset management firm belongs to several financial groups, I employ more than one group variable (I define x 1, x 2, x 3, and x 4, from larger to smaller values, in table 2-3). In the sample for this study, all the group variables for independent and foreign-capitalized asset management firms take the value 0. The estimated parameter of the group variable that is significantly positive signifies that the sales company favors investment trusts from within the group.

Commission variables, size variables, performance variables, and a variable for the number of years since the fund was established (x 13) are used as control variables.[15] For the commission variables, I use the sales company's total commissions (sales commissions + sales company's portion of trust fees, x 5), trust fees (trust company's portion, x 6), and trust fees (asset management firm's portion, x 7). For the size variable, I use net assets under management (x 8) and market share within the same Morningstar category (x 9); for the performance variables, I use both the number of stars from Morningstar (x 10) and the Sharpe ratio (for the past one year and the past three years, x 11 and x 12).

Table 2-3 shows the estimation results for the logit model. In almost every case, irrespective of industry type, the group variables are significantly positive.[16] Accordingly, assuming equal commissions, asset size, and other factors, sales companies tended to choose funds managed by firms within the group over funds from outside the group. This finding suggests the possibility that fund retailers engage in behavior that suppresses competition among providers.

Although Japan's investment trust market has been moving toward a more open architecture in recent years, some of the major banks have been increasing their reliance on funds managed by affiliates.[17] In view of the potential harm from such incestuous deals, a close eye probably should be kept on whether the trend toward consolidation within group accelerates.

15. In deciding which variables to select, I referenced Elton, Gruber, and Busse (2004), Choi, Laibson, and Madrian (2006), Del Guercio and Tkac (2001), Zhao (2005), and Bergstresser, Chalmers, and Tufano (2006).

16. This chapter reports only the estimation results from a sample including a balanced fund and a fund of funds, but the group variables for other fund categories (domestic equity, index-linked) were significantly positive overall.

17. For example, Nomura Group affiliate JOINVEST Securities handles many investment trusts from outside Nomura Group, and Nikko Cordial Group's Cordial Communications launched a fund supermarket business in October 2006.

Other Challenges

Investor education probably merits some attention. Investment trusts paying a monthly dividend—a fund category that has seen rapid growth in the last several years—provide a monthly cash flow but at a substantial sacrifice of long-term investment returns. There are lingering doubts as to whether the investors who buy such products really understand that trade-off. Maybe what Japan needs is a public-private partnership capable of implementing an investor education program that is considerably more effective, modeled after investor education programs in other countries.

Furthermore, given the large number of small-scale funds comprised by Japan's investment trust market, there also is room to consider fund mergers. The number of investment trusts with net assets below ¥1 billion was 603 at the end of December 2006, and those funds accounted for 30 percent of the total number of investment trusts. If the size of net assets becomes too small, investment performance can suffer as a result of less flexibility in making investments. If the smaller, poorly performing investment trusts attract all the attention, investors may lose interest in investment trusts. Although it also is important that the asset management companies themselves rethink their optimal size, it seems that one good way to improve investment performance and reduce fees would be to implement measures that encourage the smaller investment trusts to grow.[18]

Conclusion

The key question is whether the growth that Japan's investment trust market has delivered since 2003 is as sustainable as the growth in the U.S. mutual fund industry that began in the 1980s. Clearly the recent growth in investment trusts in Japan has been helped along not only by yen depreciation and a strong stock market, but also by structural factors such as demographic change, product innovation, broader distribution channels, and growing participation in defined contribution pension plans.

However, it is impossible to ignore the impact that markets can have on the inflow of funds into investment trusts, which probably can be attributed to mutual fund investors focusing on short-term rather than long-term returns. There also is cause for concern, from the industrial organization perspective, that investors'

18. Japan's rules on investment trust mergers are not yet fully developed (see Nomura 2007). Jayaraman, Khorana, and Nelling (2002) found that fund mergers in the United States led to better investment performance and lower fees.

choices will be narrowed and product innovation will be suppressed if incestuous transactions within the leading financial groups become the norm.

With that in mind, the key factors determining whether growth in the investment trust market can be sustained can probably be summarized as follows. The first factor concerns changes to the rules governing defined contribution pension plans, including those determining enrollment eligibility and investment selection. Both broadening eligibility and increasing maximum contributions are changes that are likely to support growth in the investment trust industry. The second factor is whether the investment trust industry is able to ensure healthy competition. If the trend toward consolidation within groups goes too far, there is a risk that competition will fail to function adequately, which would have an unfavorable impact on investors. Avoiding such a situation and (indirectly) creating greater competition among providers may require fuller disclosure of each fund's investment risks and results, thereby easing the information asymmetries between investors on one side and asset management firms and fund retailers on the other. In addition, I think that greater efforts to educate investors, along with rules changes to facilitate the consolidation of investment trusts, could have a positive impact on the development of Japan's investment trust industry.

References

Bergstresser, Daniel, John M. R. Chalmers, and Peter Tufano. 2006. "Assessing the Costs and Benefits of Brokers in the Mutual Fund Industry." Working paper (January 16). See http:// papers.ssrn.com/sol3/papers.cfm?abstract_id=616981#PaperDownload.
Choi, J. James, David Laibson, and C. Brigitte Madrian. 2006. "Why Does the Law of One Price Fail? An Experiment on Index Mutual Funds." Working Paper 12261. Cambridge, Mass.: National Bureau of Economic Research.
Del Guercio, Daniel, and A. P. Tkac. 2001. "Star Power: The Effect of Morningstar Ratings on Mutual Fund Flows." Working Paper 2001-15. Atlanta, Ga.: Federal Reserve Bank of Atlanta.
Elton, Edwin J., Martin J. Gruber, and Jeffrey A. Busse. 2004. "Are Investors Rational? Choices among Index Funds." *Journal of Finance* 59 (1): 261–88.
Jayaraman, Narayanan, Ajay Khorana, and Edward Nelling. 2002. "An Analysis of the Determinants and Shareholder Wealth Effects of Mutual Fund Mergers." *Journal of Finance* 57 (3): 1521–51.
Khorana, Ajay, Henri Servaes, and Peter Tufano. 2005. "Explaining the Size of the Mutual Fund Industry around the World." *Journal of Financial Economics* 78 (1): 145–85.
Nakagawa, Shinobu, and Tomoko Katagiri. 1999. "Nihon no kakei no kin-yushisan sentaku koudou" [Japanese Households' Portfolio Selection Behavior]. *Bank of Japan Monthly Bulletin*, December (in Japanese).
Nomura, Akiko. 2007. "Shohin rainappu gourika no shudan to shite katsuyo sareru beikoku no toushin gappei" [Mutual Fund Mergers in the U.S. as a Way to Streamline Product Lineups]. *Capital Market Quarterly* (Winter) (in Japanese).

NPO 401k Education Society and Fidelity Investments Japan Limited. 2007. "Kakutei Kyoshutsu Nenkin Mathcing Kyoshutsu Tokubetsu Houjin Zei Tou Ni Kansuru Kigyou Tantou-sha No Ishiki Chousa" [Survey on Employee's Contribution to 401k Account and Tax Considerations] (in Japanese).

Pension Fund Association. 2007. "Kakutei Kyoshutsu Nenkin Ni Kansuru Jittai Houkoku" [Survey on the Status of Defined Contribution Plans] (in Japanese).

Remolona, M. Eli, Paul Keiman, and Debbie Gruenstein. 1997. "Market Returns and Mutual Fund Flows." *FRBNY Economic Policy Review* (July): 33–52.

Thaler, Richard H., and Shlomo Benartzi. 2004. "Save More Tomorrow ™: Using Behavioral Economics to Increase Employee Saving," *Journal of Political Economy* 112 (S1): 164–87.

Wallison, Peter J., and Robert E. Litan. 2007. "Is There a Better Way to Regulate Mutual Funds?" Washington: American Enterprise Institute (April 9) (http://www.aei.org/events/type.past,filter.all,eventID.1485/event_detail.asp).

Warther, Vincent A. 1995. "Aggregate Mutual Fund Flows and Securities Returns." *Journal of Financial Economics* 39 (2-3): 209–35.

Zhao, Xinge. 2005. "Determinants of Flows into Retail Bond Funds." *Financial Analysts Journal* 61 (4): 47–59.

AJAY KHORANA
HENRI SERVAES

3

On the Future of the Mutual Fund Industry around the World

SINCE THE INTRODUCTION in 1924 of the first mutual fund in the United States, the mutual fund industry has experienced tremendous growth, not only in the United States but also throughout the world. Khorana, Servaes, and Tufano (2005) documents that at the end of 2001, the global mutual fund industry had $11.7 trillion in assets, 40 percent of which was domiciled outside the United States. A significant portion of the remaining assets were concentrated in Luxembourg ($750 billion), France ($721 billion), Italy ($360 billion), and Japan ($343 billion). By the end of the third quarter of 2007, the worldwide figure had grown to $25.8 trillion, with approximately 52 percent of all assets domiciled outside the United States. Luxembourg remains the second-largest market in the world, with assets of $2.92 trillion, followed by France ($2.22 trillion), Germany ($1.49 trillion), and Australia (first-quarter 2007 figure of $936 billion).[1]

We would like to thank Brian Reid and participants at the Brookings–Tokyo Club Seminar on the Future of the Mutual Fund for helpful discussions and comments. The views expressed herein are those of the authors and not of Citigroup Global Markets Inc.

1. See Investment Company Institute, "Trends in Mutual Fund Investing" (October 2007) (www.ici.org/stats/mf/trends_10_07.html#TopOfPage); EFAMA (European Funds and Asset Management Association), supplementary tables, "Total Net Assets in U.S. Dollars" (2007) (www.efama.org/ 60Statistics/20MoreStat/International_Statistics/intlstatsq12007suppltables/documentfile); EFAMA, "Trends in the European Investment Fund Industry in the Fourth Quarter of 2007," Quarterly Statistical Release 32 (2008).

This chapter provides an overview of the mutual fund industry worldwide and highlights our views on the industry's future evolution. A lot of our thinking relates to changes that we expect to take place in the United States; if we expect contrasting trends to emerge in other countries, we highlight them separately. This worldwide emphasis is especially important because we believe that more of the industry's future growth will occur outside the United States. Obviously it is not possible to assess the future of the industry without considering relevant facts and figures about where it currently stands; each topic therefore starts with a description of the current state of the industry with respect to that topic.

We start this chapter by summarizing some of our earlier work on the size of the mutual fund industry worldwide and the factors related to its success. We also discuss how legal and regulatory factors affect industry growth and speculate on what their effects imply for the future. We then turn to a description of methods used to sell and distribute funds, contrasting the approaches employed in different countries, and follow that with some thoughts on how the process is likely to evolve going forward. We also describe costs across funds and across countries.

We then turn to the newer types of funds that have been introduced, such as index funds, funds of funds, and hedged mutual funds. What are the costs and benefits of these funds? Will they become more important in the future?

We also review aspects of fund investor behavior. While a number of attempts have been made to show that investor behavior with respect to fund choice is fully rational, we find it difficult to support that contention. If investors are not fully rational, then funds can potentially benefit from their behavior, and we illustrate what actions funds can take in light of observed investor behavior and its implications for the future.

The chapter next sheds light on fund governance and the role of fund directors in particular. We review the work on the importance of fund directors, examining what evidence there is to indicate that governance standards affect performance; we also discuss how we expect fund boards to evolve in the future.

We then consider the tricky issue of performance. A majority of the academic research supports the view that it is not possible for fund managers to earn risk-adjusted excess returns sufficient to warrant the fees that they charge. However, recent academic work suggests that particular subsets of fund managers do exhibit persistently superior performance. We review those findings and discuss their implications for the industry's future.

We then report on concentration in the fund management industry, predicting further consolidation in the future and speculating on what it implies for investors and for the industry's future profitability. We conclude by summarizing our thoughts regarding the future of the mutual fund industry overall.

Determinants of the Size of the Mutual Fund Industry around the World

Table 3-1 provides a summary of the size of the fund industry in countries around the world in 2001, based on Khorana, Servaes, and Tufano (2005). Two conclusions emerge. First, Luxembourg, not the United States, has the largest fund industry relative to its GDP and to the size of its equity and debt market (primary securities), followed by Ireland. The ranking of Luxembourg and Ireland is attributable to the fact that they have become hubs for sales of funds across Europe; funds are set up in both countries and offered for sale in many other European countries. Their size obviously comes at the expense of industry size in the rest of Europe. Hong Kong ranks third, again because many of the funds domiciled in Hong Kong are also sold elsewhere. Fourth on the list is Australia, with a ratio of industry size to GDP of 93.4 percent (the U.S. ratio is 68.3 percent). Australia's funds are sold domestically; therefore, if we ignore cross-border sales, Australia actually has the largest fund industry in the world (using industry size relative to GDP as the measure).

Second, in many countries, the industry is very small relative to both GDP and the size of the debt and equity market, implying large future growth potential. Markets that stand out are those in China, India, Russia, and perhaps Turkey, all countries that have a relatively large GDP but only a small fund industry. If each of those markets were to grow in size to the sample median assets to GDP, it would add $97 billion in assets in China, $29 billion in India, $27 billion in Russia, and $10 billion in Turkey. While those numbers are small relative to the size of the U.S. market, they clearly are conservative estimates of the growth potential in those countries. There is little doubt that the markets will grow, even relative to GDP, but we do not believe that they will be as substantial as in the United States or much of western Europe unless a number of conditions are met. Khorana, Servaes, and Tufano (2005) discusses those conditions in great detail. In what follows, we highlight some of the study's findings and give specific examples of possible improvements to allow the industry to thrive and grow.

Typically, the industry does not flourish unless the overall quality of a country's judicial system is high. Most of the time China and Russia are excluded from studies that investigate the quality of the judicial system, but it is safe to say that at this point they would not rank high. We do have data on judicial system quality for India and Turkey. Khorana, Servaes, and Tufano (2005) computes a measure of judicial quality by summing up five measures developed by La Porta and others (1998): efficiency of the judicial system, rule of law, corruption, risk of expropriation, and risk of contract repudiation. Each variable is ranked on a scale

Table 3-1. *Mutual Fund Industry Size around the World*[a]

Country	Industry size	Industry/ primary securities	Industry/ GDP	Starting year
Algeria	0	0.000	0.000	n.a.
Argentina	3,751	0.010	0.014	1960
Australia	334,016	0.378	0.934	1965
Austria	55,211	0.142	0.293	1956
Bangladesh	5	n.a.	0.000	n.a.
Belgium	70,313	0.099	0.306	1947
Brazil	148,189	0.213	0.295	1957
Burma	0	0.000	0.000	n.a.
Canada	267,863	0.167	0.383	1932
Chile	5,090	0.042	0.077	1965
China	7,300	0.003	0.006	2001
Costa Rica	1,428	n.a.	0.088	n.a.
Croatia	384	0.024	0.019	1997
Czech Republic	1,778	0.041	0.031	1994
Denmark	33,831	0.075	0.209	1962
Ecuador	200	0.014	0.015	n.a.
Finland	12,933	0.043	0.106	1987
France	721,973	0.212	0.550	1964
Germany	213,662	0.035	0.116	1949
Greece	23,888	0.108	0.205	1969
Hong Kong	170,073	0.203	1.051	1960
Hungary	2,260	n.a.	0.044	1992
India	13,490	0.037	0.028	1964
Indonesia	764	0.007	0.005	1996
Ireland	191,840	0.823	1.856	1973
Israel	14,200	0.071	0.126	1936
Italy	359,879	0.128	0.330	1983
Japan	343,907	0.026	0.083	1965
Libya	0	0.000	0.000	n.a.
Luxembourg	758,720	4.845	39.914	1959
Malaysia	10,180	0.040	0.115	1959
Mexico	31,723	0.090	0.051	1956
Morocco	4,100	n.a.	0.125	n.a.
Netherlands	93,580	0.059	0.246	1929
New Zealand	6,564	0.071	0.132	1960
Norway	14,752	0.060	0.090	1993
Pakistan	375	0.013	0.006	1962
Peru	680	0.024	0.013	n.a.
Philippines	211	0.003	0.003	1958

(continued)

Table 3-1. *Mutual Fund Industry Size around the World*[a] *(continued)*

Country	Industry size	Industry/ primary securities	Industry/ GDP	Starting year
Poland	2,936	0.023	0.017	1992
Portugal	16,618	0.065	0.151	1986
Romania	10	0.001	0.000	1994
Russia	297	0.002	0.001	1996
Saudi Arabia	12,105	n.a.	0.068	n.a.
Singapore	7,538	0.016	0.088	1959
Slovakia	165	0.013	0.008	1992
Slovenia	1,538	0.131	0.082	1992
South Africa	14,561	0.076	0.129	1965
South Korea	119,439	0.165	0.283	1969
Spain	159,899	0.101	0.275	1958
Sri Lanka	44	0.008	0.003	1992
Sweden	65,538	0.129	0.313	1958
Switzerland	75,973	0.065	0.307	1938
Taiwan	49,742	n.a.	0.176	1984
Thailand	8,430	0.052	0.071	1995
Tunisia	471	0.027	0.024	1991
Turkey	3,000	0.023	0.020	1986
United Arab Emirates	0	0.000	0.000	n.a.
United Kingdom	316,702	0.061	0.222	1934
United States	6,974,976	0.193	0.683	1924
Uruguay	185	0.022	0.010	n.a.
Yugoslavia	0	0.000	0.000	n.a.
Median		0.048	0.088	
Mean		0.071	0.148	

Source: Based on Khorana, Servaes, and Tufano (2005).

a. The table lists the size of the fund industry at the end of 2001 (in $ millions). Only open-end mutual funds are included in the analysis. Ireland, Luxembourg, Hong Kong, and countries with no industry were dropped in calculating medians and means. See Khorana, Servaes, and Tufano (2005) for a more detailed description of the sources employed to collect these data.

from 1 to 10; a higher value implies better quality. The judicial score was 30.61 for India and 27.31 for Turkey. The U.S. score was 47.61, while all countries with a well-developed fund market scored above 40. We therefore believe that the growth potential in India and Turkey is limited unless the overall quality of their legal regime improves. However, we do not expect to see dramatic improvements in legal quality in the near future.

Khorana, Servaes, and Tufano (2005) also finds that the industry was larger when fund initiations and fund prospectuses required regulatory approval. In

India both fund initiations and prospectuses require approval, and part of an approval process is already in place in China, Russia, and Turkey.

In addition, fund management companies want to be able to start new funds quickly and at low cost. Khorana, Servaes, and Tufano (2005) finds that industries are larger in countries where the relative cost to set up a fund—computed as cost divided by average fund size—is small and where the process takes less than 120 days. The effect of setup time in particular is dramatic. Industries are about 5 percentage points smaller relative to the size of the debt and equity market and about 16 to 19 percentage points smaller relative to GDP when setup time is longer than 120 days. We find it unlikely that simply shortening the period (that is, the launch window) without making any other changes will have a dramatic effect on industry size because we believe that the setup period is just a proxy for the ease of doing business. Nevertheless, allowing funds to be established faster clearly is an important step, as long as it does not affect the quality of the review process that takes places before a fund is established. It also is important to note that a short setup period is not a necessary condition for the fund industry's success: at 225 days, the U.S. setup time is one of the longest in the world.

Finally, Khorana, Servaes, and Tufano (2005) reports that the fund industry is larger in countries that have more defined contribution pension plans. Therefore, replacing defined benefit with defined contribution plans (or adding such plans) is one way of stimulating the development of the industry. However, we believe it will take a long time before China, Russia, or Turkey will move in that direction. Poirson (2007) reports that in India efforts to establish defined contribution plans are well under way.

In sum, we expect most of the growth in the industry to come from expansion outside the United States. But if the industry is to reach its full potential, countries need to improve the overall quality of their judicial system. We believe that any such improvement is unlikely to occur in the near future, especially in those countries with the largest perceived growth potential.

How Funds Are Sold and How Much It Costs to Own Them

There are basically three channels through which funds are sold: direct sales through a fund management company; sales through a financial adviser; and sales through a commercial bank. The third channel is really a hybrid, because some banks, though not all, provide advice to customers when asked. In addition, banks usually sell their own bank-sponsored funds, although lately the choice of products has expanded to include other funds. The predominant type of distribution mechanism used varies by country. In the United States, most funds are sold through brokers or by a fund management company directly—see Berg-stresser, Chalmers, and Tufano (2008)—but banks are the primary distributors in most of continental Europe. That is due in part to the fact that for much of the history of the fund industry, U.S. banks were prevented from offering mutual funds.

We do not expect current distribution channels to undergo dramatic changes in the future; they are well established, and we expect no shifts in the supply of or demand for other distribution channels. Of course, when funds are not distributed directly by the fund management company, the distributors have to be compensated, and their fees have to be paid either indirectly, through superior performance, or directly, through reductions in other fees. However, in a careful comparison of funds sold through intermediaries and funds sold directly—see Bergstresser, Chalmers, and Tufano (2008)—funds sold through intermediaries had higher non-distribution-related fees and inferior risk-adjusted performance. Those findings notwithstanding, intermediaries will remain important in the fund distribution process because of their perceived benefits or the lack of awareness among potential customers about alternative purchase mechanisms. We discuss these issues in more detail later in the chapter when we analyze consumer behavior.

Cross-Country Sales

Some countries—Australia, Canada, Japan, and the United States among them—have created in essence a closed fund marketplace: only funds established in a particular country can be offered for sale in that country, and they are not offered for sale in other countries. In the European Union, on the other hand, funds can be sold across countries with relative ease, mainly because regulations were developed to allow it to happen. As alluded to earlier, many cross-border sales in the EU originate in Luxembourg and Ireland, while cross-border sales from other EU countries are limited. In addition, a limited number of funds have been established in tax havens—such as Bermuda, the Cayman Islands, and the Channel Islands (Jersey, Guernsey, and the Isle of Man)—and they are offered for sale in select European countries. Khorana, Servaes, and Tufano (2008) examines more than 45,000 funds offered for sale in eighteen countries in 2002 (Australia, Austria, Belgium, Canada, Denmark, Finland, France, Germany, Italy, Japan, Luxembourg, the Netherlands, Norway, Spain, Sweden, Switzerland, the United Kingdom, and the United States). The study finds that around 54 percent of the funds were offered for sale in the country in which they were domiciled; 42 percent were domiciled either in Luxembourg, Ireland, or one of the tax havens; and only 4 percent were domiciled in another European country.

We do not expect to see dramatic changes in those patterns, but we do offer other thoughts about the future:

—Cross-border sales will remain limited to Europe and some countries in Asia (through Hong Kong). We do not expect the United States or Canada to open their markets to foreign funds. That does not mean that foreign fund managers cannot sell funds in United States or Canada, but they will have to set up operations there to do so.

—Even in Europe, cross-border sales will decline in importance. In particular, sales from countries other than Luxembourg and Ireland will suffer, because part of the attractiveness of funds from Luxembourg and other tax havens comes from their ability to keep ownership of and income from the funds concealed from tax authorities. As European legislation changes, it will become more difficult to do so, thereby reducing the benefit of buying funds from these countries. Luxembourg and Ireland will suffer to a lesser degree because they will continue to benefit from EU legislation permitting cross-border sales and because they are now well-established fund hubs.

—Luxembourg's dominance over Ireland is likely to increase going forward. Of the two pan-European fund hubs, Luxembourg has always been larger; Khorana, Servaes, and Tufano (2008) reports that 7,748 fund classes were domiciled in Luxembourg in 2002 and only 1,279 in Dublin. The difference is due in part to the fact that Luxembourg was the first market to act as a hub for cross-border sales, in part because of its strict bank secrecy laws. Ireland became an entrant only relatively recently, through the establishment of the Dublin International Financial Services Centre. Fund management companies that set up operations in Dublin were given tax breaks to do so, fueling the industry's dramatic growth. However, those tax advantages have now expired, and because more of the critical mass for cross-border funds is still in Luxembourg, we have no reason to believe that the strong growth in Dublin will continue.

What Does It Cost to Own a Fund?

Investors have to pay a variety of fees when purchasing mutual funds. Broadly speaking, fees are of two types: one-time fees that are paid when an investor enters or leaves the fund (or both) and annual recurring fees. Annual fees can be further divided into two subsets: management fees and all other expenses. Management fees are revenues of the fund management company, used to pay the salaries of investment managers and other operating expenses, including advertising costs. Management fees sometimes follow a sliding scale, with fees declining as the value of assets under management increases. All other expenses are direct expenses borne by the fund, such as transfer agent fees, custodian fees, accounting fees, and audit and legal fees. They are passed on to investors, but they do not accrue to the management company. In addition, in some countries, such as the United States, management companies are allowed to include a separate charge for distribution (called a 12b-1 fee in the United States). Those fees are used by the fund management company to pay for efforts to sell, market, and advertise the fund. In practice, most, if not all, of the fees are used to compensate the financial advisers selling the fund.

Fees levied for entering the fund (front-end loads) and exiting the fund (back-end loads) accrue to the fund management company, but they also can be used as compensation for the advisers selling the funds. Back-end loads often follow a sliding scale, with fees declining as investors keep their money in the fund for a longer period of time.

There are substantial differences in fees charged across countries and across funds within a country. Khorana, Servaes, and Tufano (2008) documents various fee levels for funds offered for sale in eighteen countries at the end of 2002 (see the list of countries on p. 71), including fourteen European countries, Australia, Canada, Japan, and the United States. The authors look at management fees, total expense ratios, and total expense ratios combined with entry and exit fees (loads), assuming that investors remain invested in the funds for five years. The differences are startling. For example, equity funds offered for sale in the United States had the lowest value-weighted management fees (0.62 percent), while the fees were more than three times higher in Canada (1.96 percent). When other expenses and amortized loads were added, Australia had the lowest costs (1.41 percent), while Canada remained most expensive (3.00 percent). The differences can be explained in part by the fact that fund sizes differ across countries and that fees generally are negatively related to size. Similarly, there is a negative relation between fees and the size of the fund complex. However, the differences remain large even after taking into account measures of scale and scope. Various factors are related to the remaining fee differences, the most important of which is that fees are lower in countries with stronger investor protections. We do not expect to see dramatic shifts in the fees being charged across countries, mainly because we do not expect to see major changes in the underlying factors driving the fees.

Some specific pressures have arisen within certain countries, however. In Canada, the press has been particularly vocal about the findings presented in Khorana, Servaes, and Tufano (2008) showing that Canada is the most expensive country in the world for fund investors. Part of the reason is that distribution costs are high: the vast majority of funds in Canada are sold through advisers who have to be compensated. But, as pointed out above, management fees are high as well. The response from the Investment Institute of Canada (IFIC), which represents the Canadian fund industry, has been that investors have a preference for fund advisers; they also present arguments questioning the reliability of the research. However, Khorana, Servaes, and Tufano's response to those arguments indicates that IFIC's criticisms have little or no merit.[2] Despite the fund industry's response, some Canadian funds have started lowering their fees recently. We expect to see a further modest decline in the future.

Fee levels in the United States are quite modest when placed in an international context. Nevertheless, there has been substantial criticism of fee levels, due in part to findings in Freeman and Brown (2001). The authors compare mutual fund fees to pension fund fees and argue that while they should be similar, mutual fund fees were much higher. Freeman has testified about their study in Congress, and a statement from the New York state attorney general's office supports Freeman and Brown's arguments.[3] At the heart of the matter is the conjecture that fund management companies have not passed along economies of scale in fund management to investors. That allegation has been followed by a spate of lawsuits against fund management companies, but up to this point, most cases have been dismissed in summary judgment.

The cases have been filed under Section 36(b) of the Investment Company Act, claiming that with an increase in assets under management, fund advisers reap significant economies of scale and that the savings are not adequately passed on to fund shareholders. In a well-known section 36(b) case, *Gartenberg v. Merrill Lynch Asset Management*, the courts ruled that in order to violate section 36(b), the "adviser must charge a fee that is so disproportionately large that it bears no reasonable relationship to the services rendered and could not have been the product of arm's length bargaining."[4] A number of these cases have been dismissed in U.S. courts on the grounds that the plaintiffs failed to establish material facts to support their arguments. Some cases have gone to trial, however, and

2. "Letter to President and CEO of the Investment Funds Institute of Canada Responding to Her Comments on a Previous Draft of the Paper: 'Mutual Fund Fees around the World'" (faculty.london.edu/hservaes/ific.pdf).

3. John P. Freeman, "A Law Professor Comments on the Mutual Fund Fee Mess," statement before the Senate Governmental Affairs Subcommittee on Financial Management, the Budget, and International Security, January 27, 2004 (www.senate.gov/~govt-aff/_files/012704freeman.pdf); New York State Attorney General's Office, "Statement by Attorney General Eliot Spitzer regarding the Investment Company Institute's Mutual Fund Fee Report," 2004 (www.oag.state.ny.us/press/2004/jan/jan06b_04.html).

4. *Gartenberg v. Merrill Lynch Asset Management, Inc.*, 528 F. Supp. 1038 (S.D.N.Y. 1981), aff'd, 694 F.2d 923 (2d Cir. 1982), cert. denied, 461 U.S. 906 (1983) (Gartenberg I); *Gartenberg v. Merrill Lynch Asset Management, Inc.*, 573 F. Supp. 1293 (S.D.N.Y. 1983), aff'd, 740 F.2d 190 (2d Cir. 1984) (Gartenberg II).

Table 3-2. *Expense Ratios and Price Dispersion in the U.S. Mutual Fund Industry,*
2000

Sector	Number	Average fee (percent)	75th percentile/ 25th percentile	90th percentile/ 10th percentile
Aggressive growth	1,274	1.91	2.0	3.1
Balance growth	472	1.64	2.2	3.7
High-quality bonds	862	1.18	2.5	4.9
High-yield bonds	337	1.67	2.2	3.2
Growth and income	978	1.58	2.5	5.5
Government securities	450	1.32	2.5	4.7
Income	218	1.71	2.2	3.4
Long-term growth	1,812	1.79	2.0	3.1
Retail S&P500 Index	82	0.97	3.1	8.2

Source: Hortaçsu and Syverson (2004).

we believe that if the plaintiffs are successful, there may be some downward pressure on fees in the future.

As mentioned earlier, substantial differences in fees exist within countries for
similar fund types. Table 3-2 contains selected numbers from Hortaçsu and Syverson (2004), which explores fee differences among U.S. funds in 2000, with a particular focus on S&P 500 index funds. What stands out in this table is the wide
distribution of expenses for similar fund types. The ratio of the 75th percentile of
the distribution of fees relative to the 25th percentile is at least 2 for all sectors
listed in the table, while the ratio of the 90th to the 10th percentile exceeds 3 and
is as high as 8.2 for S&P 500 index funds. Hortaçsu and Syverson (2004) also presents two other interesting facts about S&P 500 index funds. First, the weighted
average fee for the funds actually increased over the period 1995–2000 from
26.8 basis points to 32.2 basis points. Second, the market share of the funds in the
lowest-cost quartile declined over that period from 86 percent to 75 percent, while
the market share of the funds in the highest-cost quartile increased from 1.4 percent to 4.1 percent. How is that possible, particularly given that information dissemination has improved over time, thereby reducing search costs?

The authors argue that three factors can explain the findings, and their empirical work supports their view. First, while search costs have decreased for the average investor, they have actually increased for the marginal investor because more
first-time investors have entered the mutual fund market. Second, switching costs
are an important consideration, and investors like to retain assets in funds managed by the same fund management company. Third, investors value features

other than performance, such as responsiveness to their queries. Elton, Gruber, and Busse (2004) also studies S&P 500 index funds, and the authors also note the large differences in fees charged by various funds. While they discuss rational explanations for the survival of high-cost index funds, they also entertain the possibility that the survival of such funds is possible only if investors are irrational. We discuss investor behavior in more detail later and describe how fund management companies may benefit from it.

There is one final cost element that we have not discussed: performance (incentive) fees, which are charged when performance exceeds certain prespecified benchmarks. Performance fees are not very common in the United States because since 1970 the fees have had to be symmetric (fulcrum fees), meaning that a fund management company has to reduce its fees for underperformance to the same extent that it increases its fees for superior performance. Elton, Gruber, and Blake (2003) studies incentive fees in the U.S. mutual fund industry and finds that in 1999 only 1.7 percent of all funds charged incentive fees; however, those funds controlled 10.5 percent of all fund assets. It is surprising, however, that those funds did not earn any incentive fees, on average, because they did not outperform their benchmarks. In Europe, such funds are much more common, because the fees can be asymmetric, meaning that funds may receive extra remuneration for outperformance but do not have to pay for underperformance. Sigurdsson (2007) reports that 12 percent of European equity funds have such a structure and that funds take various actions to maximize the value of performance fees.

We do not expect to see significant growth in the importance of performance fees in the United States, given their symmetric nature. However, we believe that there is room for growth of such fees in Europe because they may generate extra income for fund management companies while strengthening the perception that the objectives of the fund and the investor are aligned.

New Fund Types

Mutual funds invest in all types of assets. Some specific fund types, discussed below, have grown in importance over the past decade or so, and they are likely to continue to do so in the future.

INDEX FUNDS. Index funds mimic the performance of an underlying index. The first column of table 3-3 shows that in 2002 index funds made up a modest fraction of all funds offered in a number of countries. They were most popular in Japan, where 6.3 percent of all funds offered were index funds, and least popular in Norway, where they made up only 0.3 percent of all funds. It is possible, of

Table 3-3. *Specific fund Types by Country, 2002*[a]
Percent

Country of sale	Fraction Index Funds	Fraction Indexed Assets	Fraction Guaranteed Funds	Fraction Sector Funds	Fraction Funds of Funds
Austria	1.9	1.2	0.8	9.7	2.4
Belgium	2.1	1.1	8.7	14.2	0.9
Canada	5.1	3.1	n.a.	15.5	n.a.
Finland	1.4	1.9	0.0	20.0	1.5
France	3.1	1.6	1.2	10.0	8.6
Germany	2.5	1.5	0.6	12.9	3.1
Italy	1.3	0.5	0.6	14.0	2.7
Japan	6.3	8.8	n.a.	n.a.	n.a.
Luxembourg	1.8	1.8	2.0	19.0	2.3
Netherlands	2.1	1.7	1.1	22.0	1.5
Norway	0.3	0.3	0.1	16.0	3.5
Spain	1.0	0.8	9.8	11.6	5.1
Sweden	1.2	1.1	0.0	12.1	1.4
Switzerland	1.1	1.0	0.4	9.9	0.6
United Kingdom	1.1	1.2	0.5	7.4	3.1
United States	3.5	5.6	n.a.	13.0	n.a.

Source: Based on individual fund data provided by Morningstar, Lipper Fitzrovia, and Financial Research Corporation.

a. Table lists the fraction of specific fund types by country of sale, except for the second column, where the fraction is based on assets. In the first, third, fourth, and fifth columns, the reported fraction is computed as the fraction of fund classes offered for sale in each country that are of the specific type.

course, that there are relatively few funds but that they make up a large fraction of fund assets. However, that is not the case, as illustrated in the second column. In fact, there were only three countries where the importance of index funds increased when they were weighted by size—Finland, Japan, and the United States. We expect further, but limited, growth of the U.S. index sector, based on three factors: information on the advantages of indexing is becoming more widely available; fewer investors are novices; and a number of major players in the fund industry have reduced the management fees on their index funds. Our sense is that index funds will also gain in importance in Europe as potential investors become more informed about the benefits of indexing. However, another type of fund has emerged in Europe, guaranteed funds, which shares some of the features of index funds.

GUARANTEED FUNDS. Guaranteed funds typically are established with a limited life and the promise of a capital guarantee if held for that period. For example, a fund may have been established in 2001 with a five-year life span. It guarantees investors that they will fully participate in the increase in value of the underlying index but that if the index drops below the starting level, investors will receive their original investment, with no loss of principal. Such a strategy is financed by investing in zero coupon bonds, combined with options on the index. Given that the returns often do not include the dividends received on the index, the strategy can easily be executed with the funds received when a fund starts operations. A variation on guaranteed funds is the so-called "click fund." Such funds not only provide capital guarantees but also "click in" gains if they exceed a certain threshold. For example, if the underlying stock index increases by 20 percent over the life of the fund, those gains will be clicked in and investors will not lose them under any circumstances. As illustrated in the third column of table 3-3, guaranteed funds are extremely popular in certain European countries, Belgium and Spain in particular. Our sense is that their popularity will increase because the capital guarantee makes for an easy marketing tool. In addition, Khorana, Servaes, and Tufano (2008) finds that guaranteed funds charge lower fees than other funds with the same investment objective: total shareholder costs, which include annualized loads, are about 15 basis points lower for guaranteed funds. That also may appeal to investors. However, guaranteed funds are much more expensive than index funds, while often they just mimic the performance of the underlying index.

SECTOR FUNDS. Sector funds specialize in a particular sector of the economy and invest almost exclusively in equities. They also are very popular. The fourth column of table 3-3 shows that these specialty funds make up 10 percent or more of all equity funds in most countries, with a low of 7.4 percent in the United Kingdom and a high of 22 percent in the Netherlands. Khorana and Nelling (1997) documents that sector funds perform as well as other diversified equity funds and are not any riskier than small-cap or aggressive growth funds; the authors conclude that sector funds have a role to play in an investor's overall portfolio. We believe that such funds will maintain their popularity going forward and will be used as a portfolio optimization tool for sophisticated retail investors.

FUNDS OF FUNDS. Funds of funds are mutual funds that invest in other funds; most of the time the other funds are mutual funds as well, but they could also be hedge funds. We know very little about these investment vehicles, but as illustrated in the fifth column of table 3-3, they are quite prominent in some countries, and we believe that they deserve further study. Khorana, Servaes, and Tufano (2008) reports that these funds are substantially cheaper than regular funds with the same objective, but it is important to be aware of the fact that the underlying funds are also charging management fees. Given the dual layer of fees levied, we are surprised by their success. One possibility is that fund investors are less aware of the embedded fees. Without further study, it is difficult to make predictions regarding the future success of these investment vehicles.

HEDGED MUTUAL FUNDS. Hedged mutual funds follow strategies similar to those followed by hedge funds. Because hedge funds follow various styles, identifying them is not a straightforward exercise. Using a variety of search methods, Agarwal, Boyson, and Naik (2008) identifies forty-six U.S. mutual funds that follow hedge fund strategies. The authors did not find that the funds performed especially well relative to traditional mutual funds or hedge funds but that they did have higher expenses. Nevertheless, we believe that this type of fund will continue to grow in importance as retail investors, in pursuit of enhanced returns, seek exposure to strategies of the hedge fund type.

In sum, we believe that a number of the emerging fund types will attract a disproportionate share of new assets because of one or more of the following features: simplicity, cost, or unique product appeal. As a result, funds in traditional asset classes are likely to lose market share to these fund types. We also expect traditional mutual funds to lose some market share to hedge funds and exchange-traded funds, but we expect the losses to be limited.

The Behavior of Fund Investors

Consumers tend to choose products that maximize their utility, and how they choose mutual funds should be no different. While funds come with certain attributes that affect their perceived benefits (including the services provided by the fund management group, such as recordkeeping), we believe that the key driver of consumer choice should be a fund's expected risk-adjusted return. That return should be computed after management fees and other expenses have been deducted, and, ideally, should also take into account the tax consequences for fund investors.

Consumer Behavior

A number of academic papers cast doubt on whether fund investors behave rationally. Below is a summary of some stylized facts regarding consumer behavior in the fund industry, together with an assessment of whether such behavior may be rational, and if so, under what circumstances.

CHASING WINNERS. Funds that have performed well in the past realize large inflows, particularly star funds—that is, funds that realize the highest performance levels. In fact, what is almost a winner-takes-all phenomenon appears: the best funds get a disproportionate share of new money. See, for example, Sirri and Tufano (1998).

Is such behavior rational? There are three possible scenarios in which it may be. First, it could be rational if excess performance persists (hot hands). However, there has been relatively little evidence in the literature to support the hot hands phenomenon. The most influential study in this area is Carhart (1997), which demonstrates that there is virtually no evidence of persistence in fund returns after controlling for a variety of risk factors. The one exception in the author's research is the persistence in performance among poorly performing funds. More recently, there has been some work suggesting that certain fund and manager characteristics are associated with excess performance; we will defer a discussion of that work and its implications until later in the chapter. ·

Second, better-performing funds may receive more media attention, which reduces search costs for fund investors. However, Sirri and Tufano (1998) finds little evidence that that is the case. While media attention correlates with fund flows, the authors' evidence does not support the notion that media attention drives flows or that flows are larger for better-performing funds that have received a lot of media attention. Of course, there may be other ways to attract consumers' attention. Funds that charge high fees may be able to employ those fees in advertising, thereby reducing the search costs for investors. Sirri and Tufano's evidence is consistent with that possibility: the flow-performance relationship is especially strong for high-fee funds.

Third, even without hot hands or search costs, chasing winners could still be rational. That valuable insight comes from Berk and Green (2004), which develops a model of the fund industry consistent with a number of stylized facts. The authors' key assumption is that some fund managers may be able to earn excess returns but that as they attract more funds, their ability to deliver excess performance declines. Investors learn about managerial ability by observing past returns. Funds that have high past returns attract additional investors, but, as a result of the additional inflows, diseconomies of scale prevent fund managers from delivering superior performance on a consistent basis. That is certainly a possibility, but we are concerned about a number of other implications. When calibrating their model, Berk and Green found that if managers' funds were expanding upon initial good performance, their excess returns would have to have been 6.5 percent before fees on the first dollars invested and 5 percent after assumed management fees of 1.5 percent. We find those numbers to be quite high, but we recognize that others may have different opinions.

Fund investors not only chase winners but also focus their attention on external certification of performance by Morningstar. Morningstar rates virtually every fund in existence in the United States and in many other markets. It assigns a star ranking of from one to five stars based on three-year, five-year, and ten-year risk-adjusted performance. Del Guercio and Tkac (2008) shows that those ratings have a substantial impact on subsequent inflows and that the effect is not subsumed by returns. Khorana and Servaes (2007) finds that family market share is positively related to Morningstar ratings and that that effect is stronger than the effect of performance. Is it rational on the part of fund investors to chase Morningstar rankings? It is if such ratings have a substantial impact on search costs, but further research is required to investigate that possibility.

Overall, we find the winner-chasing behavior of consumers in the fund industry somewhat puzzling. While lower search costs or greater managerial skill combined with economies of scale may explain some of the behavior, we are reluctant to support that conclusion. In particular, we feel that the search costs have to be extremely high to justify search-cost-based arguments.

FAILURE TO WITHDRAW FROM POORLY PERFORMING FUNDS. As discussed, poor performance persists; it therefore is surprising that investors fail to withdraw their money from funds that perform poorly. Berk and Tonks (2007) reports that such funds do face substantial withdrawals if performance is poor for only one year but that the flow-performance sensitivity declines substantially for funds that continue performing poorly. They argue that many investors *do* leave poorly performing funds, but after those investors have left, the remaining investors are less sensitive to poor performance. Why? It does not appear to be rational on the part of such investors. Are they not aware of other options available, or are they merely oblivious to what happens to their funds? In either case, we do not believe that such behavior is rational.

FAILURE TO CHOOSE AMONG THE BEST OPTIONS. As discussed, in the United States there is large variation in fees among funds with the same investment objectives, even for a highly homogeneous fund category such as S&P 500 index funds. We mentioned three possible explanations for such behavior: search costs; product differentiation; and irrationality. While we feel that the first two arguments are difficult to rule out in practice, Choi, Laibson, and Madrian (2008) presents an experiment that diminishes their importance. Wharton MBA students and students from Harvard College were asked to allocate funds across four S&P 500 index funds. When provided with a prospectus that disclosed fees, 95 percent of the students failed to minimize fees. Of course, the students still had to incur search costs to find the fees in the prospectus. However, even when they were given a summary statement of fees, thereby eliminating search costs, 85 percent still failed to minimize fees. Finally, when students were provided with data on the return on the fund since its inception, a piece of information that is completely irrelevant, students actually chased funds with the best performance. Choi, Laibson, and Madrian (2008) concludes that search costs alone cannot explain investor behavior and that investors appear to value some fund attributes other than services provided by the fund management company.

UNEQUAL TREATMENT OF FEES. At least two articles suggest that investors treat different types of fees differently. Barber, Odean, and Zheng (2005) argues that investors pay more attention to fees that are more apparent, such as front-end loads, than to annual expenses. The authors find that mutual fund flows are negatively related to front-end loads but not to annual expenses. When they subdivided expenses into regular operating expenses and marketing expenses (so-called 12b-1 fees), they found that investors were less likely to buy funds with high operating expenses but more likely to buy funds with high marketing expenses. Given that operating expenses do have a negative effect on fund flows, that result does not fully support their argument. All it really says is that the marketing effort paid off.

Khorana and Servaes (2007) studies the market share of fund families. The authors find a positive relationship between loads and market share, a negative relationship between operating expenses and market share, and no relationship between 12b-1 fees and market share. Their interpretation is that loads are paid to financial advisers for selling funds and that a larger selling effort helps; operating expenses, on the other hand, reflect the price paid for the service, and funds that charge a higher price are smaller. However, if some of the fees are used explicitly for marketing (12b-1 fees), they counterbalance that effect. Thus, while all fees ultimately affect net return in a similar way, fees that are employed in sales efforts do not reduce the size of the fund management company.

ASYMMETRIC RESPONSE TO FEE CHANGES. Khorana and Servaes (2007) studies the effect of changes in fund management company expenses on their market share in the U.S. mutual fund industry. The authors find that fund families that reduced expenses gained market share in the sample as a whole and that families that increased expenses lost market share. However, that result applied only to fund families with above-average expenses. For families with below-average expenses, changing fees did not affect market share, as long as fees remained below average. Fund families can benefit from that asymmetric response on the part of fund investors.

Fund Family Response

If consumers are irrational, funds and the families that sponsor them can potentially benefit from their behavior in the following ways:

—*Promote and create top funds.* Given that winning funds attract a disproportionate amount of all new money invested in the industry, it is important for fund families to promote and create such funds. Promotion implies spending money on advertising and sales efforts. As Sirri and Tufano (1998) demonstrates, the flow-performance relationship is especially strong for high-fee funds. Funds should exercise care, however; while the relationship does hold for high-fee funds, it is not obvious that star funds can simply increase their fees in the future. In addition to the promotion of funds, families can create top funds; they have a number of methods at their disposal to do so. First, they can start many funds at the same time so that, by luck alone, one of them may turn out to be an excellent performer. The funds that perform poorly can be closed down or merged into another fund, and the surviving fund can use its own performance track record in promotions. Second, families may be able to subsidize the performance of some funds at the expense of others. Gaspar, Massa, and Matos (2006) shows that doing so is possible through preferential IPO allocations and trading among funds in the family and that it is especially relevant for high-performance and high-fee funds.

—*Take advantage of consumers' treatment of fees.* Fund families can take many actions to benefit from the failure of consumers to consider all aspects of fees. First, given the lack of sensitivity between fees and market share for low-cost fund families, families with below-average fees should consider raising their prices. Second, as discussed in Khorana and Servaes (1999), fund families could start new funds that resemble existing funds just to reset fee breakpoints to higher levels. Third, funds that have performed poorly and have seen all the smart money leave could consider raising their fees because the remaining investors appear not to be fee sensitive. Fourth, in countries where asymmetric performance fees are allowed, the introduction of performance fees can enhance revenues for the fund adviser.

—*Cash in on risk aversion.* Funds that provide a capital guarantee are relatively easy to manage, mainly because they often follow an indexed approach. While the fees on such funds are generally lower than fees for actively managed funds, they are higher than for index funds, and fund families can include such funds in their product mix to increase aggregate fees earned. Clicking in gains achieved after a certain period of time also may help.

Governance

Mutual funds in general and fund boards in particular have come under increased scrutiny in the United States, particularly in light of late trading and market timing irregularities that have surfaced at a small number of funds over the past few years.

Some believe that the actions of fund boards are influenced by investment advisers, and therefore the effectiveness of fund boards in managing the potentially divergent objectives of fund advisers and shareholders has come into question.

As mentioned earlier, one outcome of the adverse publicity has been shareholder lawsuits claiming that fund fees in the United States are excessive; however, the cross-country study of fees in Khorana, Servaes, and Tufano (2008) documents that U.S. fund fees are some of the lowest in the world. Regardless, since fee setting is an important part of the negotiations between the fund and the fund management company and one in which the board plays a vital role, board effectiveness is being examined more closely. The U.S. Securities and Exchange Commission (SEC) has initiated new rules affecting the composition of fund boards that require boards to increase the proportion of independent directors from 50 percent to 75 percent and to place an outside chairperson on the board. The new rules are being actively debated by the industry and regulators.

While this is a very U.S.-centric view of the industry, the debate has raised a fundamental issue with regard to the role and effectiveness of fund boards in general. Some question whether fund boards are even needed since external market forces can substitute for board regulation and oversight by allocating capital to better-performing (net of fees) fund complexes. In markets around the world in which investors are generally more capable of making rational capital allocation decisions, some would suggest that doing away with fund boards is a plausible scenario; see, for example, Wallison and Litan (2007). However, others argue that small investors do indeed need the protection provided by mutual fund boards that function well.

There is some empirical evidence in the United States on how board structure influences a variety of decisions that fund boards are entrusted with, including those regarding the approval of fees and fund mergers. Tufano and Sevick (1997) documents that funds with a greater proportion of independent directors levy lower fees, and Khorana, Tufano, and Wedge (2007) finds that more independent boards are quicker to arrest a fund's underperformance by initiating a fund merger. However, neither study finds any evidence to suggest that the presence of an independent chair makes the board more effective, which is a fiercely debated issue. The studies do shed some light on how board structure affects board effectiveness.

Kuhnen (2007) focuses on the importance of connections in the choice of directors and advisory firms. The author finds that directors tend to hire advisory firms (fund families) that they have worked with in the past and that when creating new funds, advisory firms offer board seats to directors with whom they have had business relationships in the past. The more connected that board members are to the management of the fund family, the higher the management fees and expense ratios. While those connections are clearly important, it is virtually impossible for investors to trace these relationships.

In light of the evidence, it is unlikely that mutual fund boards are going to become redundant any time in the near future, at least in the United States. However, we do believe that regulation and disclosure rules will be modified to make fund boards a more important shareholder protection mechanism, both in the United States and around the world.

Improvements in Assessing Skill and What It Means to Investors

As discussed previously, until the start of the twenty-first century there was a relatively broad consensus that funds could not systematically earn positive risk-adjusted returns after taking into account the fees that they charge. In addition, there was little evidence to suggest that fund and fund manager characteristics were related to performance. That consensus no longer holds. We now review some of the studies on fund return predictability, but we urge readers to be cautious when interpreting the evidence. More research is clearly warranted to determine whether these findings are robust.

One of the first studies to challenge the consensus view is Chevalier and Ellison (1999). The authors find that various fund manager characteristics, such as age and whether the manager holds an MBA, were related to performance. A lot of the effects disappeared after properly controlling for risk and expenses, but one survived: there was a positive relationship between performance and the average SAT scores of students in the universities attended by the fund managers.

More recently, Khorana, Servaes, and Wedge (2007) documents a positive relationship between the amount of personal wealth invested by fund managers in the funds that they managed and subsequent performance. Using new SEC disclosure requirements imposed on U.S. funds, the authors study the 2005 performance of all funds with manager ownership available as of December 2004, a sample covering more than 1,300 funds. They find that the average manager's investment in his or her funds was quite modest (about $97,000) but that nevertheless a strong positive relationship existed between the fraction of the fund's assets owned by fund managers and subsequent performance: for every percentage point of fund assets owned by managers, risk-adjusted performance increased by about 3 percentage points. The authors suggest that the effect is due to the incentives created by managerial ownership to work harder at beating the market, but they acknowledge that it also could have been information based. That is, managers buy more shares in their funds because they know the funds will outperform. Either way, the information is useful for investors in making portfolio allocation decisions.

Along similar lines, Cremers and others (2008) finds a positive relation between fund performance and the ownership stake of the directors of the fund.

The previous studies focus on managerial characteristics; recent studies also have considered fund characteristics and fund family characteristics. Chen and others (2004) finds an inverse relation between fund size and returns but a positive relation between family size and returns. The negative effect was most pronounced in small stocks, suggesting that liquidity may be an important driver of the relationship.

Another line of research focuses on the actual portfolio composition of the funds, which has to be disclosed only in the United States. One of the first contributions in this area is Cohen, Coval, and Pastor (2005), which examines whether the portfolio holdings of a manager match those of successful managers—the more closely they match, the more skilled the manager is in picking stocks. More important, they find that this measure can be used not only to assess skill but also to predict future performance: subsequent returns of managers in the best performance quintile were between 2.4 percent to 4.4 percent higher per year than the returns of those in the worst quintile. Wermers, Yao, and Zhao (2007) shows that that approach yields even higher returns when applied to the stocks held by the funds instead of to the funds themselves.

Kacperczyk, Sialm, and Zheng (2005), a study of industry concentration of actively managed U.S. funds, finds that more concentrated funds perform better, after controlling for risk, suggesting that managers with a more concentrated portfolio are more skilled. Kacperczyk, Sialm, and Zheng (2008) uses portfolio disclosures to compute the return on a fund, minus the return the fund would have earned had it not changed its portfolio composition since the composition was last disclosed. This return gap captures unobservable actions by funds. Kacperczyk, Sialm, and Zheng (2008) finds that the gap predicts future fund performance: the decile portfolio with the highest return gap outperforms the market by 1.2 percent a year, while the portfolio with the lowest gap generates a market-adjusted return of −2.2 percent. Finally, Cremers and Petajisto (2008) develops a new measure of portfolio management called "active share," which captures the extent to which the portfolio weights deviate from the index against which fund performance is measured. Funds with a low active share are really closet indexers—that is, they claim to be actively managed but just hold the underlying index. The authors find that this measure of active management is positively related to performance: funds with the highest active share pick portfolios that outperform their benchmarks by approximately 1.5 percent per year after fees and transaction costs are taken into account.

Cohen, Frazzini, and Malloy (2007) takes the portfolio holdings approach a step further. The authors develop a trading strategy based on the portfolio holdings of mutual funds that does not require investment in the funds themselves. Their strategy is based on an extensive study of the education networks of fund managers and corporate board members. Investing in these connected stocks (stocks of companies whose board members have a connection with fund managers) yields excess returns of up to 8.5 percent per year.

A final line of research focuses on improvements in econometric techniques to identify performance persistence. In a bootstrap analysis, Kosowski and others (2006) uncovers performance persistence for 10 percent of U.S. domestic equity fund managers, while Mamaysky, Spiegel, and Zhang (2007) shows that it is possible to identify persistent excess performance of 3.5 percent to 7 percent a year when different models for measuring fund performance are combined.

Implications for Investors

Overall, the research reviewed above suggests that various factors and techniques can be combined to identify excess performance. What do those findings imply for investors? Whether the findings discussed previously affect investors obviously depends on whether investors have access to the information in the first place and what they do with it. We believe that three groups of investors are emerging. First, *naïve investors.* These are investors who are poorly informed about fund availability and about what it costs to invest in funds, and they have no insight into the work on the predictability of returns. Instead of buying funds, they are "sold" funds, often load funds through financial advisers. In addition to the loads, such funds also charge nontrivial management fees, which have an obvious negative effect on fund performance. Naïve investors also exhibit the strongest irrational behavior: they chase past performance, they do not fully consider the impact of fees on performance, and they are most easily persuaded to invest by advertising. They also show the most interest in guaranteed funds and click funds, and they can be convinced that performance fees are necessary to motivate managers. Moreover, they stay behind when smarter money has left a fund. While such investors are important for the profitability of the fund management industry, they are in the minority, and as information becomes even more available, we expect a modest decline in their importance in the future.

Second, *informed investors.* These investors have taken more time to become informed about the various options available, and they also have a better understanding of finance and financial markets. Fees are a key determinant in their decisionmaking, but they still can be convinced that performance persists, without studying the drivers of persistence. They often allocate some of their money to index funds, while the remainder is actively managed. When performance deteriorates, they reallocate their capital. They are attracted by the promise of high returns on hedge funds, but they are not fully aware that the high management and performance fees charged in that sector may compromise performance. They find hedged mutual funds an attractive investment option, but they know little about them because the hedged mutual fund sector is too small. The success of this sector depends very much on the performance of the first few entrants, which at this point is poor. We believe that the majority of investors, who are not aware of the research findings discussed in this chapter, fall into this category.

Third, *up-to-date investors.* These investors are more up to date on the latest research and thinking in fund management and performance assessment, in particular. They can be further subdivided into two groups: *up-to-date investors with modest wealth* and *up-to-date investors with substantial wealth.* Investors with modest wealth will remain invested in mutual funds. Part of their money will be invested in the cheapest index funds available; the remainder will be allocated according to the most recent research on fund return predictability. Investors with substantial wealth will either follow a do-it-yourself approach or use private bankers that do so. The idea is to skip the mutual fund industry altogether, if possible, and to follow the investment strategies used by successful funds. Of course, some strategies rely on fund manager traits or unobservable fund actions, and they will still require investing in funds.

There is some evidence that the new money being invested is indeed smart. Gruber (1996) finds that the return earned by newly invested money in actively managed funds is higher than the average return earned by those funds, suggesting that new money is smart. However, Zheng (1999) disputes that finding using a larger sample. Of course, those findings predate a lot of research on return predictability, and conducting a study on the performance of new money invested in the fund industry today would be a worthwhile undertaking.

Consolidation in the Fund Industry and Implications for Fund Investors

Throughout the world and within countries, a large number of companies offer mutual funds. Khorana and Servaes (2007) reports that there were 525 mutual fund families offering funds for sale in the United States in 1998, up from only 167 in 1979. That is not surprising in light of the tremendous growth experienced by the U.S. industry; what is perhaps more surprising is that the fraction of the mutual fund assets managed by the top five families has not declined at all.

Table 3-4. *Concentration in the Fund Industry in Various Countries, 2002*[a]
Percent

Country of sale	Market share of three largest families	Market share of five largest families
Australia	36	47
Austria	39	46
Belgium	29	43
Canada	24	38
Finland	54	70
France	18	26
Germany	28	39
Italy	24	33
Japan	36	49
Luxembourg	30	40
Netherlands	33	45
Norway	48	63
Spain	26	38
Sweden	32	46
Switzerland	40	51
United Kingdom	24	32
United States	28	34

Source: Based on individual fund data provided by Morningstar, Lipper Fitzrovia, and Financial Research Corporation.

a. Market shares are computed based on funds offered for sale in a specific country (not funds domiciled in that country).

Khorana and Servaes (2007) reports that the top five families managed 31 percent of total assets in 1979 and 1980 and 37 percent in 1998. The figure for 2002 was 34 percent, based on Morningstar data. That evidence attests to the success of large fund families, such as Fidelity and Vanguard, in the United States. The remaining share of the market gets divided up into smaller pieces as new fund families enter. That phenomenon is not unique to the United States. Table 3-4 shows the fraction of fund assets controlled by the three- and five-largest fund families in seventeen countries, based on data from Morningstar and Lipper Fitzrovia. The figures are based on funds offered for sale in a country, which we believe is the proper definition, rather than funds domiciled in that country. The concentration ratios are very high, ranging from 18 percent in France to 54 percent in Finland for the three-firm ratio and 26 percent in France to 70 percent in Finland for the five-firm ratio.

While it is very difficult to study the actual profitability of mutual fund operations—see, for example, Huberman (2007)—we believe that it is safe to assume that size is a critical driver of efficiency. However, given that concentration ratios already are extremely high, we do not expect much consolidation to happen at the national level among the larger players; however, there clearly is room for consolidation among the smaller players. We therefore expect the large players to maintain their positions, while consolidation among smaller players will have only a minor effect on concentration at the national level.

There has been substantial international consolidation, however. For example, when we study the ten largest asset managers domiciled in the seventeen countries listed in table 3-4, we find that Deutsche Bank and Fidelity enter the list in five countries and Axa, Citigroup, DGZ-Dekabank, Fortis, and Nordea enter the list in three countries. Much of that consolidation has come through acquisition, although some firms have grown abroad by starting new operations in a country. We believe that it will be virtually impossible to enter a mature market as a start-up without remaining a niche player, but that strategy is still possible in developing markets. In addition, to enter the EU market, a firm has only to acquire a management company with a presence in one country to allow it to distribute funds to most member states. Luxembourg remains of key importance in that regard. Even in developing markets, we believe that acquisition may be the fastest way to establish a market presence.

We do not expect fund investors to enjoy the benefits of increased consolidation in the form of lower fees. Our sense is that any improvements in efficiency will go to the management companies' bottom line. However, that prediction has not been formally tested using past mergers and so is very speculative.

Conclusion

The future of the fund industry worldwide is healthy. In many countries, the industry is still poorly developed, and with the right regulatory impetus, there is room for a lot of growth: China, India, Russia, and Turkey are important in that regard. In many developed markets, the industry is quite mature, and while funds are being offered by a very large number of organizations, a large fraction of the market is captured by just a few companies. That applies to virtually all markets in North America and western Europe. We expect to see further consolidation in the industry among smaller fund management companies and in terms of cross-border mergers between financial institutions active in the fund industry.

We expect some pressure on fees but believe that the overall effect will be small, because a lot of investors are not fully aware of the effect of fees on performance and because fees can be used in selling efforts. Fund families have succeeded in differentiating their product offerings so that investors focus on elements besides

fees and performance. Continued innovation in fund types will help fund families in that regard. However, sophisticated investors will continue to demand low-
fee products, many of them indexed. They also will use more recent developments in the work on performance persistence to identify top-performing funds.
It is possible, however, that increased inflows into those funds will affect the predictability of their performance.

There is some evidence that improved fund governance has affected decisionmaking in some circumstances, but we would urge regulators not to impose further governance standards without a careful study of their costs and benefits. We
believe that outside the United States, consumers would be better served by more
disclosure of fees and expenses and their effect on performance. We believe that
more transparency will ultimately benefit the industry.

References

Agarwal, Vikas, Nicole M. Boyson, and Narayan Y. Naik. 2008 (forthcoming). "Hedge Funds
for Retail Investors? An Examination of Hedged Mutual Funds." *Journal of Financial and
Quantitative Analysis.*

Barber, Brad M., Terrence Odean, and Lu Zheng. 2005."Out of Sight, Out of Mind: The
Effect of Expenses on Mutual Fund Flows." *Journal of Business* 78 (6): 2095–2120.

Bergstresser, Daniel, John M. R. Chalmers, and Peter Tufano. 2008 (forthcoming). "Assessing
the Costs and Benefits of Brokers in the Mutual Fund Industry." *Review of Financial Studies.*

Berk, Jonathan B., and Richard Green. 2004. "Mutual Fund Flows and Performance in Rational Markets." *Journal of Political Economy* 112 (6): 1269–95.

Berk, Jonathan B., and Ian Tonks. 2007. "Return Persistence and Fund Flows in the Worst-
Performing Funds." Working Paper 13042. Cambridge, Mass.: National Bureau of Economic Research.

Carhart, Mark M. 1997. "On Persistence in Mutual Fund Performance." *Journal of Finance* 52
(1): 85–110.

Chen, Joseph, and others. 2004. "Does Fund Size Erode Mutual Fund Performance? The Role
of Liquidity and Organization." *American Economic Review* 94 (5): 1276–1302.

Chevalier, Judith, and Glenn Ellison. 1999. "Are Some Mutual Fund Managers Better than
Others? Cross-Sectional Patterns in Behavior and Performance." *Journal of Finance* 54 (3):
875–99.

Choi, James J., David Laibson, and Brigitte C. Madrian. 2008. "Why Does the Law of One Price
Fail? An Experiment on Index Mutual Funds." Working Paper. Yale School of Management.

Cohen, Lauren, Andrea Frazzini, and Christopher Malloy. 2007. "The Small World of Investing: Board Connections and Mutual Fund Returns." Working Paper 12261. Cambridge,
Mass.: National Bureau of Economic Research.

Cohen, Randolph B., Joshua D. Coval, and Lubos Pastor. 2005. "Judging Mutual Fund Managers by the Company They Keep." *Journal of Finance* 60 (3): 1057–96.

Cremers, Martijn, and Antti Petajisto. 2008 (forthcoming). "How Active Is Your Fund Manager? A New Measure That Predicts Performance." *Review of Financial Studies.*

Cremers, Martijn, and others. 2008 (forthcoming). "Does Skin in the Game Matter? Director Incentives and Governance in the Mutual Fund Industry." *Review of Financial Studies.*

Del Guercio, Diane, and Paula A. Tkac. 2008 (forthcoming). "Star Power: The Effect of Morningstar Ratings on Mutual Fund Flow." *Journal of Financial and Quantitative Analysis.*

Elton, Edwin J., Martin J. Gruber, and Christopher R. Blake. 2003. "Incentive Fees and Mutual Funds." *Journal of Finance* 58 (2): 779–804.

Elton, Edwin J., Martin J. Gruber, and Jeffrey A. Busse. 2004. "Are Investors Rational? Choices among Index Funds." *Journal of Finance* 59 (1): 261–88.

Freeman, John P., and Stewart L. Brown. 2001. "Mutual Fund Advisory Fees: The Cost of Conflicts of Interest." *Journal of Corporation Law* 26 (3): 609–73.

Gaspar, José-Miguel, Massimo Massa, and Pedro Matos. 2006. "Favoritism in Mutual Fund Families? Evidence on Strategic Cross-Fund Subsidization." *Journal of Finance* 61 (1): 73–104.

Gruber, Martin J. 1996. "Another Puzzle: The Growth in Actively Managed Mutual Funds." *Journal of Finance* 51 (3): 783–810.

Hortaçsu, Ali, and Chad Syverson. 2004. "Product Differentiation, Search Costs, and Competition in the Mutual Fund Industry: A Case Study of S&P 500 Index Funds." *Quarterly Journal of Economics* 119 (2): 403–56.

Huberman, Gur. 2007. "Is the Price of Money Managers Too Low?" Discussion Paper 6531. London: Center for Economic Policy Research.

Kacperczyk, Marcin, Clemens Sialm, and Lu Zheng. 2005. "On the Industry Concentration of Actively Managed Equity Mutual Funds." *Journal of Finance* 60 (4): 1983–2011.

———. 2008 (forthcoming). "Unobserved Actions of Mutual Funds." *Review of Financial Studies.*

Khorana, Ajay, and Edward Nelling. 1997. "The Performance, Risk, and Diversification of Sector Funds." *Financial Analysts' Journal* 53 (3): 62–74.

Khorana, Ajay, and Henri Servaes. 1999. "The Determinants of Mutual Fund Starts." *Review of Financial Studies* 12 (5): 1043–74.

———. 2007. "Competition and Conflicts of Interest in the U.S. Mutual Fund Industry." Working paper. Georgia Institute of Technology and London Business School.

Khorana, Ajay, Henri Servaes, and Peter Tufano. 2005. "Explaining the Size of the Mutual Fund Industry around the World." *Journal of Financial Economics* 78 (1): 145–85.

———. 2008 (forthcoming). "Mutual Fund Fees around the World." *Review of Financial Studies.*

Khorana, Ajay, Henri Servaes, and Lei Wedge. 2007. "Portfolio Manager Ownership and Fund Performance." *Journal of Financial Economics* 85 (1): 179–204.

Khorana, Ajay, Peter Tufano, and Lei Wedge. 2007. "Board Structure, Mergers, and Shareholder Wealth: A Study of the Mutual Fund Industry." *Journal of Financial Economics* 85 (2): 571–98.

Kosowski, Robert, and others. 2006. "Can Mutual Fund 'Stars' Really Pick Stocks? New Evidence from a Bootstrap Analysis." *Journal of Finance* 61 (6): 2551–95.

Kuhnen, Camelia. 2007. "Social Networks, Corporate Governance, and Contracting in the Mutual Fund Industry." Working paper. Northwestern University.

La Porta, Rafael, and others. 1998. "Law and Finance." *Journal of Political Economy* 106 (6): 1113–55.

Mamaysky, Harry, Matthew Spiegel, and Hong Zhang. 2007. "Improved Forecasting of Mutual Fund Alphas and Betas." *Review of Finance* 11 (3): 359–400.

Poirson, Hélène K. 2007. "Financial Market Implications of India's Pension Reform." IMF Working Paper 07/85. Washington: International Monetary Fund.

Sigurdsson, Kari. 2007. "Asymmetric Performance Fees in European Mutual Funds." Working paper. London Business School.

Sirri, Erik R., and Peter Tufano. 1998. "Costly Search and Mutual Fund Flows." *Journal of Finance* 53 (5): 1589–1622.

Tufano, Peter, and Matthew Sevick. 1997. "Board Structure and Fee-Setting in the U.S. Mutual Fund Industry." *Journal of Financial Economics* 46 (3): 321–56.

Wallison, Peter J., and Robert E. Litan. 2007. *Competitive Equity: A Better Way to Organize Mutual Funds.* Washington: American Enterprise Institute.

Wermers, Russ, Tong Yao, and Jane Zhao. 2007. "The Investment Value of Mutual Fund Portfolio Disclosures." Working paper. University of Maryland.

Zheng, Lu. 1999. "Is Money Smart? A Study of Mutual Fund Investors' Fund Selection Ability." *Journal of Finance* 54 (3): 901–33.

COMMENT

The Future of the Mutual Fund
Industry in the United States
and Elsewhere

BRIAN REID

FORECASTING IS AS much an art as a science, a fact reflected in chapter 1, by Paula Tkac, and in chapter 3, by Ajay Khorana and Henri Servaes. At times we may be lucky enough to know in advance about a future event, such as a presidential election or, in the case of Tkac's chapter, the retirement of the baby boom generation. But even then, the specifics of how that event will unfold are generally very uncertain. Inevitably, looking to the future requires examining the past in order to ground our forecasts of uncertain events. Tkac and Khorana and Servaes therefore build their analyses on backward-looking frameworks, while spending ample time on contemporary realities to devise a framework for their views of the future. The frameworks that they build, however, rely on relatively disparate underlying models and focus on different aspects of those realities. This chapter compares the outlooks of Tkac and Khorana and Servaes, examines their underlying models, and gives independent comments on where the future might take the mutual fund industry.

There are three important differences between Tkac's chapter and the chapter by Khorana and Servaes. The first lies in the structure of their frameworks. Tkac's is largely parsimonious, working from the epigraph of the chapter, which observes that "the only thing that stays the same is change." Tkac sees change, but in her treatment of events and trends in the present and recent past, that change does not diverge from but continues what has to some degree already begun. Relying on a crucial and certain exogenous event, the coming retirement of the baby

95

boom generation, Tkac frames her arguments principally within the context of competition among profit-maximizing firms to meet investor preferences. In slight contrast, Khorana and Servaes provide a framework with many more parameters, but one in which they still include firms maximizing profits. Rather than focus on one defining event, they look instead at a variety of factors—including investor behavior, fund governance and performance, and product innovation—and at how changes in each of those areas could affect the U.S. and the international industry.

Second, within their frameworks, the authors paint different pictures of investors and what drives their demand for financial products. Tkac believes demand to be driven by a variety of consumer preferences based primarily on demographics; for example, the rise in annuities that Tkac predicts will be driven by baby boomers seeking income in retirement. Khorana and Servaes see consumers as not fully rational; because of that, understanding how investor characteristics will influence mutual fund demand is not so simple a task. In general, the two authors find that although price sensitivity differs among investors, the wealthiest investors have the most options.

The third difference lies in how firms operate given the nature of consumer demand. For Tkac, in the spirit of her parsimonious model, profit-maximizing firms compete to meet investor needs, and there is little to complicate a standard general equilibrium model. In the case of Khorana and Servaes, firms maximize profits by seeking to exploit investors' lack of full rationality. For example, a firm can take advantage of the investors' tendency to try to pick winners by aggressively promoting or creating top funds, which are more likely to draw their attention.

Delving more deeply into Tkac's model and conclusions, it becomes evident that product innovation driven by investor demand can be broken down into specific categories of preferences. Risk-return preferences have driven demand for 130/30 funds; moral and ethical concerns are driving demand for socially responsible funds; lower fee preferences have promoted the growth and popularity of index funds and ETFs (a claim in dispute with some of the conclusions of Khorana and Servaes); and finally, a desire for advice has made target date funds one of the fastest-growing products in the industry.

Some of these innovations are a result of the demographic shifts that Tkac highlights, and baby boomers in particular have driven innovation by demanding new methods of decumulation. But as baby boomers decumulate their assets, the mutual fund industry must prepare itself to serve the post-boom cohort that will soon enter its prime saving years by designing new products to suit their preferences. Public policy also has played a role in investor demand and product innovation. Because innovation favors large firms, large mutual fund organizations as well as other large financial service organizations are most likely to be the future innovators.

The approach of Khorana and Servaes is to parameterize a model that examines aspects of less than fully rational investors. They posit that while the key driver of consumer choice should, under usual assumptions of rationality, be a fund's risk-adjusted return and not any additional services offered, that does not appear to be the market reality. The authors see this as a profit-making opportunity for funds. Promoting and creating top-performing funds, taking advantage of how consumers perceive fees, and profiting from consumers' risk aversion are all potential strategies for exploiting that opportunity.

But Khorana and Servaes also are more specific; they categorize as well as parameterize investors' lack of full rationality. The forecast implied by their model relies principally on the categorical differentiation of consumers by wealth and relative degree of rationality. Those termed "smart investors" include both the wealthy and the moderately well-off. The wealthy, who have more substitutes for mutual funds (hedge funds, ETFs, SMAs, and so forth) at their disposal, are the most price sensitive, and they will leave mutual funds due to their price sensitivity. The moderately well-off, who will stay with mutual funds but who have a relatively educated and discerning eye, will invest in index funds and chase returns by following new research on return predictability. Investors that the authors classify as "informed" will seek out hedged products, but they will create little pressure on industry fees. "Naïve investors" also will do little to exert fee pressure, but they will continue to represent exploitable profit opportunities. In time, the fund industry increasingly will be left with less informed and less price-sensitive investors.

While the model of Khorana and Servaes does not assume investors' full rationality, it does have important defining assumptions. One is that there is no learning on the part of investors or agents; another is that there are no reputation effects of fund actions. Also implicit in the model is that there is minimal market pressure from price-sensitive investors. As a result, there is no incorporation of a profit-motivated response to recapture price-sensitive investors. Khorana and Servaes also examine the role that economies of scale will play in the industry. Despite finding evidence that economies of scale will drive industry concentration higher, their forecast does not predict any resulting downward pressure on prices, because of the tendency of firms to act at times like monopolists.

The key to Khorana and Servaes's argument about investor irrationality is a collection of studies and experiments relating to mutual fund fees. Choi, Laibson, and Madrian (2008), which analyzes an experiment involving MBA students at Wharton and students at Harvard who failed to pick the lowest-priced S&P 500

indexed mutual fund, is cited as evidence that even groups that we would collec-
tively deem "smart investors" do not always properly identify the lowest-priced
funds among similar choices. The authors also cite evidence from one of their
own 2007 papers. They note a positive relationship between loads and market
share, even though they find a negative relationship between operating expenses
and market share. They further note that there is evidence that investors appear
more tolerant of fee increases in funds that have lower prices to begin with.

   However, despite such evidence of irrationality with respect to fees, there is
other strong evidence that consumers act with the kind of rationality that is usually assumed in modeling the industry. Data from the Investment Company Institute (ICI) show that for stock funds, actual fees as a percentage of assets have
declined 54 percent since 1980.[1] In 1980 actual fees as a percentage of assets stood
at 2.32 percent; by 2007, they were hovering at just over 1 percent (1.07 percent).

   Much of that reduction reflects growing demand for lower-cost funds. Furthermore, it appears that investors tend to favor S&P 500 indexed funds with
expense ratios of less than 0.2 percent. Investor asset flows in S&P 500 indexed
mutual funds showed in 2006 that 82 percent of total assets held in funds with
expense ratios below 0.2 percent and net new cash flow of 79 percent went into
those same low–expense ratio funds. In fact, 71 percent of net new cash to funds
has gone to funds whose operating expenses are in the lowest quartile. Most categories of funds (bond, aggressive growth, growth and income, international
equity, and so forth) have shown at least 50 percent of net new cash going into
funds having expense ratios in the lowest quartile. Only sector funds, with 28 percent of total net new cash flows going to the lower-expense funds, are an exception to that finding. In total, only $86.67 billion of the $1.82 trillion of net new
cash has gone into funds with operating expense ratios in the top quartile. That
represents a mere 5 percent.

   In addition to consumer preferences regarding funds and their fees, Khorana
and Servaes rely on consumer preferences regarding brokerage fees to further their
argument of investor irrationality. Bergstresser, Chalmers, and Tufano (2008) is
cited because it provides evidence that financial advisers assisting investors do not
select funds with superior before-fee performance. The challenge for the researchers is that they cannot cleanly identify all funds that advisers select for their
clients. Instead they identify as funds sold by brokers only those that include broker compensation as part of the fund's fee structure. In practice, financial advis-

---

1. Investment Company Institute, "Fees and Expenses of Mutual Funds" *Fundamentals* 16, no. 3 (June
2007) (www.ici.org/fundamentals/fm-v16n2.pdf).

ers can and do sell funds that do not include their compensation in the fund fees. But an even greater challenge for the researchers is that they cannot determine other motives that investors may have for using the services of an adviser.

Investor demand for a broader set of financial services is another difference between Tkac's model and that of Khorana and Servaes. The latter divorces financial services from mutual funds in that its does not include a demand for services in consumption functions. Tkac, on the other hand, examines mutual fund distribution channels, noting the importance of financial service bundling and an outlook that sees growth in bundling. When looking at mutual fund distribution channels and the influence of brokers and fees on consumer preferences and demand, it is important to understand how investors hold mutual funds. Especially important is where investors hold mutual funds outside of retirement plans, because those funds represent approximately 68 percent of the market.

What's striking is how heavily investors rely on professional advisers when they hold their shares outside of defined contribution (DC) plans. Nearly half of investors in this group use *only* professional financial advisers, while a further 33 percent couple professional advice with other sources. Only 14 percent use sources other than professional financial advisers exclusively.[2] Financial advice is not cheap, and from the perspective of Khorana and Servaes, such use of advisers is more evidence of irrationality. Because they fail to include financial services in their model of consumer demand, the authors do not consider the services of advisers as relevant to their fees. Surely investors may purchase mutual funds directly from fund companies, thus avoiding relatively substantial fees for advice; however, investors may choose to use financial advisers for reasons that do not necessarily violate rationality.

To analyze why investors choose to use advisers, the ICI conducted a study in 2006 that asked what the "major" reason for using a financial adviser was, inviting multiple responses. In general, the responses tended to reflect the idea that financial advisers provide the expertise that consumers demand. More specifically, the top reasons that shareholders looked to advisers were for explanations of various investment options, help with asset allocation, help with making sense of a total investment picture, and help in making sure that they were saving enough to meet their financial goals. There are slight differences in the responses of those investors who identify the adviser as the lead decisionmaker and those who identify themselves (or who indicate that the role is equally shared); nevertheless,

2. Investment Company Institute, "Ownership of Mutual Funds through Professional Financial Advisers," *Fundamentals* 14, no. 3 (April 2005) (www.ici.org/pdf/fm-v14n3.pdf).

responses of both types of investors provide evidence that investors do not violate rationality simply by using financial advisers because they feel that they are getting services beyond the mere buying and selling of mutual funds.

Though they never explicitly contradict each other, the chapters of Tkac and Khorana and Servaes take slightly different approaches to the question of the future of the mutual fund industry. While they do not arrive at disparate conclusions, they do focus on different aspects of the future through the different lenses provided by their models. Because of that, there is room to combine the two analyses in an effort to develop an integrated framework.

In building such a framework, it is essential to keep Tkac's model of the firm, in which the firm seeks to maximize profits by decreasing production costs and creating new products and services that investors want. Given that Khorana and Servaes note the important role of wealthy investors and their price sensitivity, it seems prudent to modify their model so that in the new framework, profit-maximizing firms seek to attract profitable large accounts. It's also important to allow mutual funds to devise strategies to retain or even attract more lucrative investors rather than assume that they will flee to hedge funds, ETFs, or the like. In addition, it's necessary to remove the assumption of monopoly pricing power in the new framework, given the low level of market concentration currently in the fund industry and the concentration of flows and assets to lower-cost funds.

Working with a known future exogenous event, in this case the demographic shift brought about by retiring baby boomers, provides the context crucial to developing this amalgamated framework. There is little doubt that this shift will have consequences for a variety of industries, including mutual funds and financial services in general. And because of the role that financial services play in mutual funds, a further step needed in developing this framework is to relax Khorana and Servaes's assumption that risk-adjusted returns are the only driver of consumer demand and instead incorporate financial services into the demand function. Although Khorana and Servaes do provide evidence that investors may not be fully rational, evidence presented earlier in this comment suggests that their assumption may not in fact be the best way to model investor behavior. Imposing time consistency and reputation effects and allowing for heterogeneity in price sensitivity, as do Khorana and Servaes, also are integral features of the new framework. Combining the models of Tkac and Khorana and Servaes in such a way can provide a more accurate and comprehensive picture of the future of the mutual fund industry.

In examining the models and predictions of Tkac and Khorana and Servaes as well as in formulating a more comprehensive framework and analyzing data that call into question the assumption of investors' irrationality, in particular with regard to fees, this analysis makes some predictions of its own. First and foremost, the evidence points to the fact that investors seek advice and that they are willing to pay for it. It seems likely that if preferences for advisory services are incorporated into the model of consumer demand, industry competition will not only affect fees but also drive firms to design new products to deliver help and advice to investors in a less costly system. One current example of this is the target-date fund, which provides a lower-cost means of offering investors asset allocation advice and periodic rebalancing of account balances. Popular already, this product and others like it will be an important component of future industry growth.

Although it's important not to ignore financial services in the future of the mutual fund industry, fees matter nevertheless. In the future, pricing pressure from within as well as outside the industry will continue to reduce the realized cost of investing in mutual funds, leading to squeezing of profit margins. That already has begun and is likely to continue into the immediate future. The squeezing of profit margins will entail further industry consolidation and the proliferation of smaller firms that will perform more specialized functions. Although this analysis predicts industry consolidation, it also predicts that economies of scale will lead to lower prices, in contrast with Khorana and Servaes, who agree with the former but not with the latter prediction. Finally, market forces are likely to continue to drive investors to the least costly options among the more commodity-like products such as index funds.

Pricing pressures will result also in further demutualization of funds, which will entail low-balance fees, transaction-related fees (payment for liquidity), and further segmentation of large and small investors. And just as consumer demand for help and advice will drive product innovation within the industry, firms themselves will continue to build and expand their information and advice offerings at ever-lower costs to investors.

With the certain and substantial demographic shift that is coming, new methods of accumulation and decumulation based on demographic trends also will be an important part of the industry's future. Many of the solutions to demographic shifts will come in the form of product innovations; however, innovations in financial service offerings also can provide options to investors who are considering their accumulation and decumulation strategies. Decumulation is of primary importance to the retiring baby boomers; therefore, funds seeking to compete will respond with flexible, cost-effective products to assist in decumulation. But with the boomers moving through the market and into a phase of greater decumulation than accumulation, the industry must meet the needs of the next generation of savers if it wants to continue its strong growth.

The future is always uncertain, even with logical and well-researched predictions. By comparing the models that Tkac and that Khorana and Servaes used to construct their outlook on the future, this analysis has combined aspects of each model and posited a likely course for the future of the mutual fund industry. There seems ample reason to expect new product innovations in the future, in addition to lower fees and a greater proliferation of products and services designed to meet the investment and income needs of investors who value help and advice in addition to the ability to buy and sell mutual funds.

COMMENT

The Future of Mutual Fund Regulations in the United States

PETER WALLISON

THE PURPOSE OF the research that Bob Litan and I conducted on the subject of mutual fund regulation was to understand and address the very broad
distribution of expense ratios in the U.S. mutual fund industry. As shown in figure 1, which represents 811 class A equity mutual funds, the distribution is
extremely wide, almost 300 percent. That is the case even after we removed the
highest and lowest 3 percent in order to eliminate outliers. This puzzled us a little because the mutual fund industry is supposed to be competitive, and in most
competitive industries the dispersion of pricing is much narrower.

The SEC has also been concerned about this phenomenon over the years. In
response, it adopted a theory suggested by scholars at the Wharton School in
1966. The idea suggested by the Wharton scholars was that there was a conflict
of interest between the manager of the fund, on one hand, and the fund and its
shareholders, on the other, and that the only way to address the conflict was to
make the directors of mutual funds more independent of their investment managers. The directors would then negotiate fees more aggressively with the manager, and that in turn would bring fees down.

Examining the evidence presented in figure 1, I believe that you would call this
theory a failure. The directors might be reducing fees, but the distribution of
expense ratios—which I will call "pricing"—in the industry doesn't look very
competitive. Nevertheless, some might argue that although there is a wide dis-
parity of expense ratios for these 811 funds, close to half of all shareholders are in

Figure 1. *Distribution of Expense Ratios of Class A Shares of U.S. Equity Mutual Funds (811 Funds)*

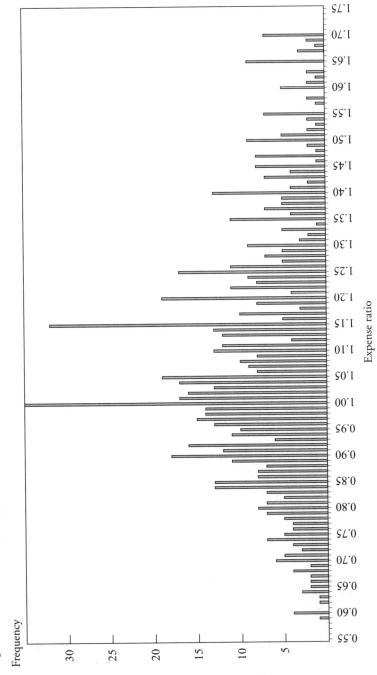

Source: Morningstar (www.morningstar.com [December 7, 2006]).

some very large funds that are run by very large management companies and that the pricing of those managers is actually more competitive.

However, if you look only at the value funds, growth funds, and blend funds of the ten largest U.S. fund families in panels A, B, and C of table 1, you still see very substantial disparities in expense ratios. Another compelling fact for us was the dispersion of pricing in the S&P index funds. If you examine the expense ratios of those funds, net of rule 12b-1 fees, there is also an exceedingly wide distribution, which again you would not expect to find in a competitive market (table 2).

There are a lot of reasons why fund price distribution might be so wide, and many have already been presented in the preceding chapters. Investors may be uninformed, they may not fully understand the information that they're given, or they may not always be presented with the information that they should have. However, many of those arguments seem hard to credit, since there is nothing about the mutual fund market that makes it different from markets in which equally uninformed customers somehow manage to cause prices to converge. A distribution as wide as the one in the mutual fund market does not fit with what you would expect to find in a truly competitive market.

Accordingly, we attempted to develop a hypothesis that would explain the distribution, and we concluded that the board's method of addressing the issue of fees and expenses is the problem. Consider yourself what you would do if you were on the board of directors of a mutual fund. How could you get a real sense of whether the manager was charging too much in fees? The only practical way is to look at the manager's profit, and that is how most boards appear to do it. If the manager is earning very high profits, it's probably charging too much to the fund. But looking at the profit fosters a cost-plus pricing system, similar to what you see with electric utilities. Utility commissions usually look at the utility company's profit percentage and try to control that. But as virtually every economist who has looked at this practice has noted, examining the profit percentage creates very little incentive for the utility to cut costs, because when it cuts its costs it raises its profit percentage, and that causes the utility commission to reduce its prices so as to bring the profit percentage back into line with what the commission thinks is reasonable.

The same explanation can be applied to the observed stickiness in the expense ratios of the mutual fund business. That is our hypothesis—that expense ratios do not reflect competition because each mutual fund board is in effect a mini utility commission. Mutual fund managers have no incentive to cut costs and raise their profits because that will only cause mutual fund boards to insist on cutting fees to bring the profit percentage back into line with what the board thinks is reasonable.

The next question is how to formulate a test of that hypothesis. One method is to look at the mutual fund industry outside the United States. We chose to look at

Table 1. *Expense Ratios of Representative Large-Cap Funds of the Ten Largest U.S. Fund Families*[a]

Fund Family	Fund and Ticker Symbol	Expense Ratio
Panel A Growth Fund		
Fidelity Investments	Fidelity Blue Chip Growth (FBGRX)	0.64
Vanguard Group	Vanguard Morgan Growth (VMRGX)	0.39
Capital Research & Management	American Funds AMCAP A (AMCPX)	0.65
Franklin Templeton Investments	Franklin Capital Growth A (FKREX)	0.95
Columbia Management Group	Columbia Large Cap Growth A (LEGAX)	1.11
J. P. Morgan Chase & Co.	JPMorgan Large Cap Growth A (OLGAX)	1.24
Morgan Stanley	Morgan Stanley Focus Growth A (AMOAX)	1.01
OppenheimerFunds/MassMutual	Oppenheimer Equity A (OEQAX)	0.80
TIAA-CREF	TIAA-CREF Growth Equity (TIGEX)	0.45
Federated Investors	Federated Large Cap Growth A (FLGAX)	1.45
Panel B Blend Fund		
Fidelity Investments	Fidelity Fund (FFIDX)	0.56
Vanguard Group	Growth & Income (VQNPX)	0.37
Capital Research & Management	No representative fund	. . .
Franklin Templeton Investments	Franklin Growth A (FKGRX)	0.94
Columbia Management Group	Columbia Large Cap Enhanced Core A (NMIAX)	0.75
J. P. Morgan Chase & Co.	JPMorgan Disciplined Equity A (JDEAX)	0.85
Morgan Stanley	Morgan Stanley Dividend Growth Securities B (DIVBX)	0.75
OppenheimerFunds/MassMutual	Oppenheimer Main Street A (MSIGX)	0.92
TIAA-CREF	TIAA-CREF Growth & Income (TIGIX)	0.43
Federated Investors	Federated Capital Appreciation A (FEDEX)	1.22
Panel C Value Fund		
Fidelity Investments	Fidelity Equity-Income II (FEQTX)	0.62
Vanguard Group	Vanguard Equity-Income (VEIPX)	0.31
Capital Research & Management	American Funds Investment Company of America A (AIVSX)	0.55
Franklin Templeton Investments	Franklin Equity Income A (FISEX)	0.93
Columbia Management Group	Columbia Large Cap Value A (NVLEX)	0.96
J. P. Morgan Chase & Co.	JPMorgan Value Opportunities A (JVOAX)	1.07
Morgan Stanley	Morgan Stanley Value A (VLUAX)	0.97
OppenheimerFunds/MassMutual	Oppenheimer Value A (CGRWX)	0.99
TIAA-CREF	No representative fund	. . .
Federated Investors	Federated Equity-Income A (LEIFX)	1.11

Source: Morningstar (www.morningstar.com [October 17, 2006]).
a. Data are as of October 17, 2006.

Table 2. *Fees, Expense Ratios, and Assets of Selected S&P 500 Index Funds*[a]
Percent except where stated otherwise

Fund and ticker symbol	Front-end load	Manage-ment fee	12b-1 fee	Expense ratio net of 12b-1 fee	Assets (billions of dollars)
Schwab S&P 500 Index Investor (SWPIX)	0.00	0.09	0.00	0.37	8.1
T. Rowe Price Equity Index 500 (PREIX)	0.00	0.15	0.00	0.35	7.5
Dreyfus S&P 500 Index (PEOPX)	0.00	0.25	0.00	0.50	3.7
Gartmore S&P 500 Index A (GRMAX)	5.75	0.13	0.25	0.25	3.5
MainStay S&P 500 Index A (MSXAX)	3.00	0.24	0.25	0.48	1.7
Morgan Stanley S&P 500 Index A (SPIAX)	5.25	0.12	0.24	0.38	1.2
Principal Investors Large Cap S&P 500 Index A (PLSAX)	1.50	0.15	0.15	0.49	1.0
Munder Index 500 A (MUXAX)	2.50	0.12	0.25	0.41	0.9
DWS S&P 500 Index A (SXPAX)	4.50	0.05	0.25	0.41	0.7
State Farm S&P 500 Index A Legacy (SLIAX)	5.00	0.20	0.25	0.55	0.6
Legg Mason Partners S&P 500 Index A (SBSPX)	0.00	0.25	0.20	0.39	0.5
United Association S&P 500 Index II (UAIIX)	0.00	0.10	0.05	0.12	0.4
AIM S&P 500 Index Inv (ISPIX)	0.00	0.25	0.25	0.60	0.2
UBS S&P 500 Index A (PSPIX)	2.50	0.20	0.25	0.70	0.2

Source: Morningstar, (www.morningstar.com [December 22, 2006]).
a. Data are as of December 22, 2006. All funds have a minimum initial investment of $2,500 or less.

the United Kingdom in particular. The United Kingdom has a legal system more or less like ours, a fairly competitive system, and it does not have boards of directors approving mutual fund expense ratios. In the United Kingdom, the advisers themselves establish what the expense ratios are in competition with one another.

In the United Kingdom, the distribution of fees is much narrower than it is in the United States (figure 2). The distribution in the United States is 300 percent, even after the outliers are removed. In contrast, the United Kingdom shows a distribution of about 90 percent. That indicates that in a market in which there is

Figure 2. *Distribution of Expense Ratios of U.K. Equity Mutual Funds (456 Funds)*

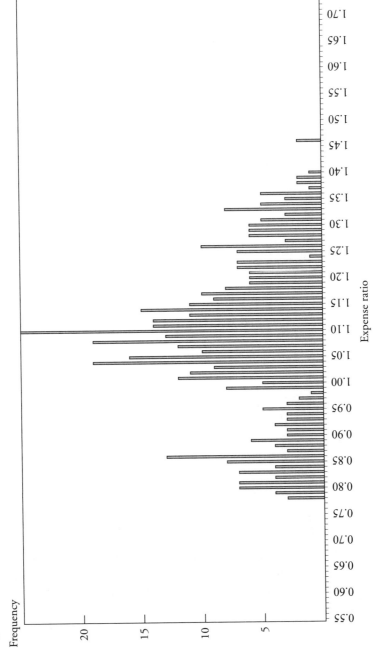

Source: Investment Management Association (from Lipper Fitzrovia data) (December 2005).

Table 3. *Asset Weighted Average Total Expense Ratios of Equity Funds of U.S. Advisory Groups That Sponsor Funds in Both the United States and United Kingdom*
Percent

Company	U.S. funds	U.K. funds
Company A	0.86	1.72
Company B	1.02	1.65
Company C	1.09	1.62
Company D	1.14	1.64
Company E	1.24	1.68
Company F	1.41	1.71

Source: "A Comparison of Mutual Fund Expenses across the Atlantic," Lipper Fund *Industry* Insight Reports, September 2005. The data for the individual companies are not shown in the report but were provided by Lipper.

no involvement in fee setting by a board of directors, competition itself produces a much narrower distribution. Therefore, we attempted to find other examples that would confirm the results that we obtained by looking at the United Kingdom in relation to the United States.

The first example that we found were data from Lipper, which show the expense ratios of six very large U.S. mutual fund firms, identified only as A, B, C, D, E, and F. These firms offer funds in both the United States and the United Kingdom. Again, in the United Kingdom, boards of directors are not involved in setting fees, consulting on fees, or in any way participating in the decision-making regarding fees. Looking at the fees from these six large firms, we saw that in the United Kingdom the fees were separated by about 10 basis points, whereas in the United States they were separated by as much as 50 or 60 basis points (table 3).

That provides further evidence, if a competitive environment yields a narrow fee distribution, that a competitive environment is not present in the U.S. mutual fund industry. What is occurring in the United States is that boards of directors are using a cost-plus system, reducing or eliminating the incentives of mutual fund managers to cut their fees.

A final example is the distribution of fees charged by money management firms for what are called "basic account strategies." These are sets of hypothetical portfolios that the firms sell to retail brokers as the basis for their clients' separate accounts. In many cases, the basic account strategies are produced by the same investment advisers who are advising mutual funds. But again, in this case there is no intervention in any way by a board of directors. As a result, you can see a much narrower range of costs, reflecting what you would expect to see in a competitive market (figure 3).

So, our prescription for the regulation of mutual funds in the future, as outlined in our book *Competitive Equity*, is to eliminate the boards of directors of mutual funds.[1] A more limited step would be to eliminate the role of boards in setting fees and retain boards to deal with the conflicts of interest that arise in managing mutual funds. But eliminating the role of boards in fee setting would benefit investors by creating a competitive environment in which fees and expense ratios would be much lower.

Wouldn't better information for investors result in more price competition? A lot of emphasis has been placed on what investors actually know—the kind of information that they have—but that really isn't the crucial question. The key question is marginal cost. When a business has identified its marginal cost, it prices for one dollar more than its marginal cost. Any sales that it makes at that price are profitable. The customer that the business is trying to attract is not the uninformed customer. Informed investors are quite price sensitive, and they are interested in having information and in buying at the lowest possible cost—and therefore in paying the lowest fee for the services of the investment adviser.

Those are the people that the investment advisers in a competitive environment would be working for, just like in selling laptops or any other competitive business. I don't know very much about laptops. I know that there are differences among them, but they're all priced within a relatively narrow range because there are people who pay a lot of attention to the quality of a laptop and to its various features and technical capabilities. Manufacturers are looking for the last marginal customer, the one who will pay slightly more than their marginal cost of producing the last laptop, and for that reason you and I and every other non-expert is the beneficiary of the competition for these customers among laptop manufacturers.

How would eliminating boards promote price competition? Price competition is what we all should be looking for in the mutual fund industry. And if we got it, I think we would see a much narrower range of fund prices, and those prices would come down a lot faster than they have in the past. In effect they would not be so sticky. In a cost-plus environment, there is a lot of stickiness. The boards in effect discourage the investment advisers from reducing their fees. Let's look at some hypothetical numbers as an example.

Let's assume that you are an investment manager who has $1 billion dollars in assets under management. You have a 1 percent expense ratio and a 20 percent

---

1. Peter J. Wallison and Robert E. Litan, *Competitive Equity: A Better Way to Organize Mutual Funds* (Washington: AEI Press, 2007).

profit. Your profit in that case is $2 million: $1 billion multiplied by 1 percent, multiplied by 20 percent. However, if you manage to reduce your expense ratio to 80 basis points, your profit goes down to $1.6 million.

Now, it could be that you will attract so much more business at 80 basis points that your profit will not actually be reduced. But that's a risk, and you know that once you've reduced your expense ratio, you're not going to be able to go back to the board and request a return to the original fee. The board simply won't let you do it.

In addition, reducing your expense ratio also has the effect of increasing your profit percentage. And the boards don't like that because, under section 36B of the Investment Company Act and rulings on various lawsuits, boards may have to explain in litigation why it is that they are allowing the manager to earn a greater profit percentage than in the past.

If boards were eliminated entirely, what would happen? Marginal cost pricing would take effect. Some of these advisers would note that their marginal cost was much lower than the pricing of their competitors, and they would cut their prices quite substantially. Then they would seek to attract investors by advertising their new, lower price.

There are a variety of things that you can say about how investment companies are pricing their mutual funds. One of the reasons that we've presented this argument is that we would hope that researchers would go back to the data to determine whether our hypothesis is correct.

Although the dispersion of pricing in the United Kingdom is narrower, aren't expense ratios higher? Actually, expense ratios in the United Kingdom are not higher. Initially it looked to us as though the U.K. fees were higher, until we discovered that a 50 basis point rule 12b-1 fee was included in our original analysis. If you look at the dispersion in the United Kingdom (figure 3), it's between about 80 basis points and 140 basis points. If you look at the dispersion in the United States, it's between 60 basis points and 170 basis points. That is, of course, eliminating outliers as specified earlier. The midpoint of the U.K. dispersion is very much in line with the midpoint of the dispersion in the United States.

Loads were subtracted from the calculation of fees in both the United Kingdom and the United States. It is true that loads in the United Kingdom tend to be higher than those in the United States; however, our analysis was primarily concerned with the dispersion of management fees and expenses as opposed to loads.

It could be that the cost to the investor to buy a fund is higher in a system that has no boards and lower in a system that has independent boards, but you would have to explain why that is the case. My knowledge of the distribution system in the United Kingdom is not sufficient to know whether fund managers there are

Figure 3. *Distribution of Fees Charged by Money Management Firms for Basic Account Strategies Used in SMAs*[a]

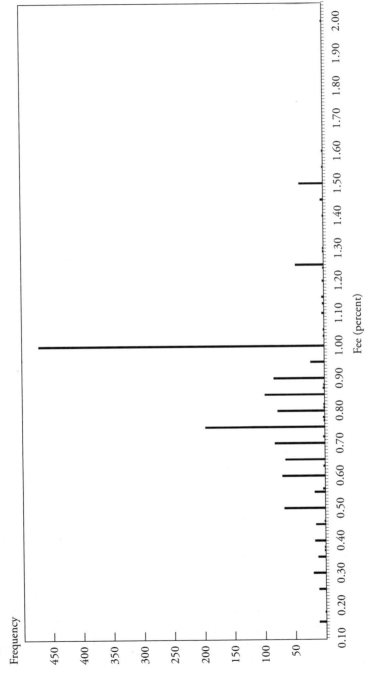

Frequency

Fee (percent)

Source: Morningstar, Morningstar Principia Separate Accounts (December 2006).
a. 1,462 strategies.

making up for their more competitive-looking fees through some kind of load system or whether distribution is done independently.

The only way to really test our hypothesis is literally to allow it to happen in the United States and observe the results. We recommend that that be done on an optional basis. We are not recommending that all boards be eliminated but that managers be given the option to offer funds without boards. It's impossible to know the results until the experiment is run.

If we were to add back all the loads and all of the rule 12b-1 fees into our 811 class A share funds, the price distribution would be even wider. We did not examine other evidence of competition in the United Kingdom beyond the dispersion of fees. The fact that six U.S. funds were offering shares in the United Kingdom too and that substantial fee differences existed between the countries seemed very indicative of competition being present in one market and not the other. However, our analysis did not go any further than that.

Why don't directors encourage managers to compete on price by cutting costs? As an adviser's profit percentage rises, directors are forced into a defensive position. They have to explain why it is that they allowed profits to rise. So, it really does create a very difficult situation for an adviser who really wants to cut his fees and see if he can earn more by attracting more investors. That, in essence, is our major thesis here.

COMMENT

The Future of Mutual Fund
Regulation in the United States:
Another View

ALLAN S. MOSTOFF

I HAVE BEEN ASKED for my view of the future of mutual fund regulation in the
United States. In addressing this subject, I suggest that we start with an understanding of where the industry is today and why it has achieved widespread
investor acceptance.

There can be no doubt that the U.S. mutual fund industry is one of the great
financial success stories of recent history. Starting as a modest accommodation by
investment counselors to the financial needs of small investors more than seventy
years ago, the acceptance of the mutual fund—as both an efficient investment
vehicle and a profitable service for advisers to offer—quickly took hold. Since
then, of course, industry growth has been explosive, to the point that mutual
fund investment assets now rival those of other financial institutions.

Today, investors entrust more than $11 trillion to the industry.[1] Much of that
success is due to the genius of the idea itself. Few investments can provide diversification and professional management as easily and efficiently as a mutual fund
can, in particular for retail investors who are saving for their retirement, their
children's education, and all their other financial goals.

These remarks are my personal views and do not necessarily represent those of the Mutual Fund Directors Forum, its members, or its staff. In preparing them, however, I benefited from the valuable assistance
of my colleagues at the Forum, and particular thanks are due to David Smith and Carolyn McPhillips.
1. See Investment Company Institute, "Trends in Mutual Fund Investing: August 2007," September
27, 2007 (http://www.ici.org/stats/mf/trends_08_07.html).

But the industry does not owe its spectacular success to the ingenuity of the mutual fund concept alone. Investors would not have entrusted their wealth and financial well-being to mutual funds unless they had significant confidence in the safety of their assets and in the motivation of their fund managers.

To what is that trust attributable? History has demonstrated time and again that investment managers cannot be relied on to manage investors' money unchecked. For compelling evidence of the need for effective oversight of fund managers, one need only look to the numerous abuses that occurred in the infancy of the U.S. industry during the 1920s and 1930s; the scandal in Europe and the United States in the 1960s of the unregulated Fund of Funds Ltd., a Canadian investment company, and its sponsor, IOS Ltd.; and, most recently, the U.S. fund scandals that occurred earlier in this decade.

Although money managers and their clients have a common interest in the growth of the clients' assets under management, few would argue today against the proposition that there also exist real and potential conflicts between money managers and their clients that need to be monitored on a day-to-day basis. In the mutual fund industry, those conflicts include—but certainly are not limited to—the setting of fees charged to a fund, the risk of self-dealing whenever a fund does business directly with its investment manager or one of the manager's affiliates, the manner in which fund assets are spent to support distribution of its shares, the use of soft dollars and other issues related to whether funds receive best execution on trades in their portfolios, and the challenge of fair valuation of fund assets.

Because of the risk that a mutual fund's investment manager will resolve conflicts in its favor rather than in a manner consistent with its fiduciary obligations to the fund's shareholders, the key to the continued success of the mutual fund industry, from the perspective of both investors and fund managers, has been a regulatory system that facilitates maintaining and increasing investor trust. I am convinced that this central goal should—and will—drive the future of fund regulation.

In the United States, from the inception of the mutual fund regulatory structure in 1940 onward, an essential technique relied on to meet the challenge of maintaining investor trust in the face of fund manager conflicts has been the empowerment of independent directors. They are the fund shareholders' first line of defense in the necessary monitoring of conflicts and overseeing the relationship of their fund with the fund's investment manager.

At this point, we might well pause and ask why Congress and the Securities and Exchange Commission (SEC) have consistently looked to an independent board of directors as a means of protecting mutual fund investors. Similarly, why does the industry itself embrace the concept of effective management oversight by an independent board of directors as a key to maintaining investor confidence? Although the regulatory scheme of the Investment Company Act is quite pervasive and somewhat complex, why is much of its effectiveness based on the assumption that independent fund directors are an effective and efficient way to oversee conflicts and respond to problems so that they are resolved in the best interests of fund shareholders?

The answer seems apparent. First, just as the mutual fund structure allows investors to pool their assets to acquire professional money management and the benefits of a diversified portfolio, it also enables fund shareholders to elect and rely on a board of directors to represent their interests in negotiating with—and overseeing—their fund manager. Large institutional investors committing significant amounts of money to professional money managers certainly expend resources and effort on monitoring those managers. Similarly, small investors are able to do the same thing within the umbrella of the mutual fund. By pooling their buying power they can, in effect, hire and rely on a board of directors to represent their best interests in dealing with their investment manager.

Second, "regulation" by directors is both more efficient and more flexible than other potential approaches. For all but the smallest segment of the mutual fund industry, the costs associated with directors—not just their fees, but also the expenses that they incur in conducting meetings, hiring consultants and other professionals, and so forth—are modest in terms of overall fund assets. In addition, because directors remain involved with the funds that they oversee on an ongoing basis, they are well positioned to respond nimbly to issues—and opportunities—that arise. The creativity and flexibility that independent directors provide have allowed fund managers and the SEC to utilize the exemptive provisions of the Investment Company Act and work together to create a highly innovative fund management industry—an industry that today offers such products as money market funds and exchange-traded funds that could not have been imagined at the time that the regulatory structure was first put in place.

Moreover, unless recognition of the special need for mutual fund investor protection is to be abandoned, the most obvious alternative to independent director oversight is the approach used in other areas of financial services such as banking regulation—implementation of a detailed regulatory system combined with large numbers of government inspectors and examiners engaged in continual oversight and monitoring of the regulated entities' activities. While such an oversight system can be effective, it is much more expensive—and a far greater taxpayer burden—than independent director oversight, the cost of which is borne by the fund shareholders who benefit most directly from it. Further, such a detailed regulatory regime does not easily allow for flexible, creative, and proactive responses to issues and problems that arise.

In sum, I believe that investor trust in the mutual fund industry, a critical key to the industry's phenomenal success, is based on the current regulatory structure, an integral component of which is an independent board of directors obligated to exercise reasonable business judgment in acting as fiduciary for shareholders. The widespread acceptance of the effectiveness of this approach is demonstrated by both the industry's extraordinary growth and its general unwillingness to entertain serious discussion of significant changes to the existing regulatory framework.

Going forward, I am convinced that the mutual fund industry, the SEC, and Congress will be unwavering in their agreement that fund shareholders are best served by continuing to entrust fund boards with responsibility for oversight of their investment managers.

At the same time, however, I recognize that there is no one "correct" regulatory approach to achieving constructive board oversight of fund management. With that objective foremost in mind, I expect that the regulatory structure will experience continued refinement in ways intended to enhance board effectiveness.

For example, whatever the resolution of the current debates surrounding the proposals for independent chairs and supermajorities of independent directors, the importance of fund director independence all but ensures that those basic issues will be regularly analyzed and reexamined.[2] Indeed, the future success of the overall mutual fund regulatory structure depends on its continued review and the identification and elimination of any impediments that it may create to the flexible exercise of reasonable business judgment by fund directors.

I believe that both the industry and the current state of boardroom independence and dynamics are mature enough to allow for safely looking for ways to eliminate regulations and approaches that have a tendency to push directors away from a purer exercise of their reasonable business judgment. Consider, for example, the so-called *Gartenberg* factors that today govern a board's approach to negotiating a management fee with the fund's manager.[3] Broadly speaking, the directors' goal in the process is to agree on a fee that represents what would otherwise be obtained in arms-length negotiations—that is, a management fee that is both

2. See, for example, *Investment Company Governance*, Investment Company Act Release No. 26520 (July 27, 2004) [69 *Federal Register* 46378 (August 2, 2004)]. See also *Investment Company Governance, Request for Additional Comment*, Investment Company Act Release No. IC-27600 (December 15, 2006) [71 *Federal Register* 76618 (December 21, 2006)].

3. See *Gartenberg v. Merrill Lynch Asset Management, Inc.*, 694 F.2d 923 (2d Cir. 1982).

competitive in the marketplace and a fair reflection of the quality of services obtained from the fund manager.

The *Gartenberg* cases require, among other things, that directors not only evaluate the nature and quality of the services provided by the fund's investment manager and assess the fund's investment performance, but also that they consider factors such as management's profitability and the existence of economies of scale. In recent years, the SEC has reemphasized the importance of all of the *Gartenberg* factors by requiring that directors address each factor when they explain to fund's shareholders why they chose to renew the management contract. In today's complex industry, however, one can well question the wisdom of this approach.

Although consideration of profitability may be central to an investment manager's business model, it is not clearly related to whether the manager has charged a fund a fair price for the services provided. For example, the profitability of a highly inefficient manager may seem acceptable even if the overall price for that manager's services, viewed in the context of the marketplace, is too high. Likewise, a focus on profitability may work to the disadvantage of a highly efficient manager and make the manager less interested in advising mutual funds.

In addition, emphasizing lists of factors, as the *Gartenberg* decision does, can result in a "check the box" approach to critical decisions that inhibits the ability of fund boards to exercise their business judgment. Fortunately, most fund boards do not operate in that manner—they recognize that relying too heavily on investment manager profitability might actually impede their ability to exercise reasonable business judgment. Looking to the future, it may well be time to reexamine whether strict and formalistic adherence to each of the *Gartenberg* factors currently inhibits fund boards from making decisions that are in the best interests of shareholders.

Another example ripe for reexamination is rule 12b-1, which governs use of fund assets to pay for distribution costs. Many commentators have noted that the factors emphasized in the current regulation—factors that were first put in place in the early 1980s—are outdated and should be revised to reflect the current nature of the fund marketplace.[4] But as the SEC continues to reexamine rule 12b-1, it appears that the best approach may be to move away from a factor-based approach, with the objective of freeing directors to use their own judgment to determine when using fund assets to pay for distribution is a wise use of shareholders' money.

4. See, for example, *Unofficial Transcript of Division of Investment Management 12b-1 Roundtable,* June 19, 2007 (http://www.sec.gov/news/openmeetings/2007/12b1transcript-061907.pdf).

In a system that emphasizes the importance of directors' business judgment, it is essential, of course, that directors have the tools and resources necessary to exercise that judgment in an informed way. The SEC's recently adopted requirement that all funds have a chief compliance officer (CCO) who reports directly to the board is a most significant step in that regard.[5] The CCO, who typically is on site at funds on a daily basis, can play an important role in identifying and highlighting issues that require board attention. Properly employed, the CCO enables directors to take a step back and focus on critical issues without becoming enmeshed in the detailed day-to-day operations of the funds that they oversee.

As the role of the CCO evolves, I expect it to continue to grow in importance and further facilitate the ability of fund boards to focus on issues of critical importance to fund shareholders. For example, the CCO could ultimately have a pivotal role in reducing the overwhelming amount of paper that directors currently receive—paper that too often compels directors to attend to less important details at the expense of the issues that are most important to shareholders. In addition, the CCO could also have a role in the monitoring of such things as routine affiliated brokerage or reports on the implementation of a fund's 12b-1 plan, again freeing directors to focus on more important issues. To achieve these and similar objectives, it will, of course, be imperative for the SEC and the mutual fund industry to focus on—and resolve—issues that have the potential to compromise the CCO's independence, including the CCO's compensation, the reporting structure within the fund, and the scope of the CCO's responsibility.

Finally, it may be useful to look at the role of shareholder litigation in the context of mutual fund regulation. Private litigation can play an important role in ensuring fund investor protection—it can be the ultimate check on the actions of fund management and, indeed, on the actions of the directors themselves. However, current shareholder litigation challenging management fees tends to focus on whether, from a process standpoint, the directors have worked through all the *Gartenberg* factors and whether they have successfully ingested all of the voluminous materials provided to them in the course of their annual review. That approach drives directors to the same sort of "check the box" form of oversight described earlier, which does not seem to be in the best interest of shareholders. Private litigation might better serve its function as the ultimate check if courts focused, as they do in other corporate contexts, on whether the directors acted

---

5. See Rule 38a-1(a)(4) under the Investment Company Act of 1940. See also *Compliance Programs of Investment Companies and Investment Advisers*, Investment Company Act Release No. 26299 (December 17, 2003) [68 *Federal Register* 74714 (December 24, 2003)].

independently and in good faith in exercising reasonable business judgment on behalf of fund shareholders.

What then is the future of mutual fund regulation in the United States? The fund industry is, as noted, highly successful. That success can be attributed in large degree to the wisdom of the regulatory regime that underpins it, a key to which is reliance on an independent board of directors to act exclusively on behalf of shareholders in the oversight of their funds and of their fund manager's performance. For this regulatory scheme to continue to be successful as the fund industry grows even larger, more complex, and ever more important to the financial well-being of U.S. investors, the SEC, legislators, and others must continue to focus on enabling fund boards to act independently on behalf of their shareholders and avoid regulations that unnecessarily restrict directors from exercising discretion. If that approach is taken, I have every reason to believe that the fund industry will achieve even greater success in the future.

Ingested by T-Rex:
How Mutual Fund Investors and Their
Retirements Fall Prey to Obsolete Tax
and Regulatory Policy

HAROLD BRADLEY

The fund industry, which appears to be competitively structured, shows signs of oli-
gopoly—or as the GAO phrased it in its 2000 report—"monopolistic competition."[1]

O NE STEPS IN dangerous waters when asked to comment on whether
mutual fund fees are competitively established. It's not quite as dangerous
to suggest that the complexity of today's regulatory environment impedes competition. An analysis of "monopolistic competition" depends on several key variables and
assumptions. Even a veteran of nineteen years in the mutual fund industry like me
finds it difficult to elucidate the fees and their complicated structure. Is the focus on
unified fee companies, where the expense ratio and the management fee are equivalent? Or is the focus on the alphabet soup of distribution fees that can seriously
impact long-term portfolio returns depending on the distribution channel used by an
investor? Wide variance exists among fees charged by broker-dealers, who restrict the
list of mutual funds to be included on their distribution platforms and then collect a
partial fee reimbursement under rule 12(b)-1. Broker-dealers can assess those pay-to-
play fees as a front-end commission load, a back-end load, or a level load paid for asset
allocation advice—making long-term returns quite varied for an essentially identical

---

1. Peter J. Wallison and Robert E. Litan, *Competitive Equity: A Better Way to Organize Mutual Funds*
(Washington: AEI Press, 2007).

portfolio of securities. Some suggest that an oligopoly of distribution firms dictates pricing for most of the industry, as five retail brokerage firms (wirehouses) are said to command 80 percent of the market share for investors who use financial advisers or brokers. What I see clearly in this fog of industry price-setting practices is that mutual fund boards are trying to do what market mechanisms do better—and mutual fund pricing today is neither straightforward nor efficient for investors.

Further clouding the issue, both broker-dealer regulations and "customer protection" rules derived from the Investment Company Act of 1940 perversely inhibit performance incentive fees, which would better align investor fees with fund performance and asset allocation advice. Increasingly, institutional investors like the Kauffman Foundation utilize separate account-pricing strategies that reduce fees paid for management services when performance is poor but ratchet up fees asymmetrically for managers who consistently deliver excess returns against market benchmarks.

Finally, a conversation about mutual fund fees should include the cost of trading securities and the use of client commissions to pay research bills under the safe harbor created by rule 28(e) in the 1975 Amendment to the Securities Exchange Act. Those charges are not part of the expense ratio reported to investors. Therefore, investors cannot understand the extent of harm to their returns from the persistent diversion of their commissions into the "safe harbor," given current record-keeping and reporting requirements. Leaders at the Securities and Exchange Commission (SEC), notably former chairman Arthur Levitt and current chairman Christopher Cox, girded for battle several times over recent years to fix this persistent leaching from investors. Proposed rulemaking supported from the bully pulpit has been stymied each time by industry interests looking for ways to hide fees paid by investors.

The conclusion by Litan and Wallison that poor corporate governance may be contributing to higher fees for investors is undeniable. With legions of consultants and advisers helping to prepare cost-justification studies for fund management companies—and the limited time that shareholder boards have to master post-doctorate levels of pricing strategy—investors and their representatives are simply outmanned. Fund timing scandals earlier in this decade prompted the SEC to place greater emphasis on the ritual dance between trustees and advisers at annual 15(c) meetings, when boards are required to approve management contracts. In 2005 the SEC asked that trustees disclose in reports to shareholders their rationales for ratifying contracts, in detail and with specificity. Board members are now justifiably terrified about personal liability and excessive-fee lawsuits.

Lawyers guide the 15(c) discussions and work to establish pricing strategies that reflect the so-called *Gartenberg* factors. One finance professional told me that lawyers set management fees today, often contravening armies of marketing statisticians analyzing competitive frameworks. To beat a class action excessive-fee lawyer, investment advisers rely on a 1982 court ruling that examined six criteria, known as the *Gartenberg* factors in the section 36(b) world, including

—the profitability of the fund's fees to an adviser

—the reasonableness of fees when compared with those of similar funds

—whether fees reflect economies of scale as the assets grow within a fund.

Those same criteria—used to repel excessive-fee litigation—are now firmly embedded in the oversight process used by board trustees when approving fees. Repelling charges of excessive fees seems to be a very different standard from ascertaining whether investors are paying reasonable fees. Board members have the chore of reconciling the 1940 Investment Company Act, the 1975 Amendment to the Securities Exchange Act, and the *Gartenberg* factors while adequately understanding hidden "off balance sheet" costs to investors through commissions and 12(b)-1 fees—which are not part of the expense ratio. That task is simply impossible.

The consultants and intermediaries engaged in this process do not work for free. Investors cannot be well served by boards constrained by rigid requirements and the assertiveness of the fee litigation crowd. As one 15(c) veteran commented to me: "It's a muddy area, and our job was to make it muddier." Does it really surprise anyone, given these considerations, that the pricing practices of the mutual fund industry closely resemble those of cost-plus home builders, as argued in *Competitive Equity?* Even a cursory review of the costs associated with annual 15(c) meetings—and those of repeating cycles of excessive-fee lawsuits—suggests to me that it's time to allow competitive market forces to set fees.

Unified fee companies exist in a kind of permanent purgatory because directors apply the same *Gartenberg* criteria used by companies that separate specific "manage money" fees from other fund expenses. The unified fee company is the only structure that rewards managers for efficiently managing costs. An investor pays only a single price for all services, including money management; the unified fee is the expense ratio. If the manager does not efficiently manage the costs of the organization, profit margins decline. Under the absurd conventions of today's dance, the efficiently managed unified fee company must justify the incremental gains in margin, defeating the fee structure that is best aligned with investor interests.

Finally, a fund company with a strong performance history and sizable assets under management has absolutely no incentive to experiment with new fee structures, like fulcrum fees. Performance-based fees might work well on niche products or those that are unable to soak up large amounts of assets without compromising investment returns. At the same time, investment company executives fear mercurial boards that, without adequate investment backgrounds, might implement the broad application of experimental strategies and significantly harm firm profitability. That inhibits any innovation in fee structures that might possibly be perceived as a threat to the organization's "greater economic good."

The *Gartenberg* Lens

My role here is to comment on the general conclusion that the mutual fund industry does not have vigorous price competition and to assess the efficacy of the regulatory framework, based on my experience. As neither a lawyer nor an economist, I express an investor's view about the complex issues surrounding important *Gartenberg* factors used by trustees to assess the reasonableness of fees.

Perpetual Fat Margins for the Mutual Fund Industry

The first key consideration involves proper evaluation of the *profitability of the fund's fees to the adviser*. Industry data over almost twenty years show persistence of profit margins of between 25 percent for inefficient performers and 50 percent and more for institutional money managers. Such persistence of "fat" margins provides additional evidence for the theory that pricing is not competitive in the industry. A recent roundtable hosted by BoardIQ reported "unanimity among the panel about the difficulty of measuring profitability, particularly on a fund-by-fund basis . . . but the important thing is whether the enterprise is successful."[2] The mutual fund industry was built on a foundation characterized by economic cross-subsidies. Almost every successful money management organization reaps outsized benefits from one or two large funds that pay most of the fixed costs for money managers, including costs for new fund creation, customer service, and asset gathering. Investors with large account balances subsidize early stage investors eager to begin investing at affordable costs. As a result, most fund companies traditionally provided no product-level profitability analysis, focusing instead on the financial statements of the adviser and the transfer agent. I'm told some fund companies choose to focus primarily on investor-class shares, thereby ignoring the 12(b)-1 fees paid by investors for advice that they receive from third-party distribution agents and the ultimate impact on investor returns. In most cases, the distribution channel has little or no impact on the "manage money" margins of an investment company.

2. BoardIQ, "Break the Boilerplate: Key Strategies for Evaluating Fund Advisory Fees," December 2007 (www.BoardIQ.com).

Reasonableness of Fees and the Change in Industry Structure

When the *Gartenberg* decision was published, the structure of the industry was entirely different from what it is today. The structural changes that have occurred complicate *an understanding of the reasonableness of fees when compared with those of similar funds.* The title of this comment, "Ingested by T-Rex," references the decades-long consolidation of money managers by large holding companies affiliated with dominant retail brokerage firms. Concomitant with this trend, technology improvements in the early 1990s allowed for the emergence of new, efficient distribution platforms referred to as NTF (no transaction fee). Suddenly, a single brokerage firm could array no-load, load, third-party, and proprietary fund products on the same platform. Formerly "no load" firms willingly rebated a portion of account servicing fees—30 or 40 basis points—to the brokerage firm in order to be included on the list.

The emergence of NTF platforms enabled independent advisers to assemble mutual fund investing strategies by using best-in-class products available through discount brokerage firms; wirehouse strategies relied on more expensive proprietary brands. In the mid-1990s, regulators found that some broker-dealers harmed investors by encouraging brokers to sell higher-margin "house" products instead of better-performing non-house brands. Wirehouses, in turn, expanded their offerings and eliminated sales incentive programs that often rewarded brokers for selling house brands rather than better-performing funds available from third-party managers. This trend accelerated as Morningstar's rating of fund performance, combined with faster and faster network technologies, eliminated the long-standing differentiation between no-load investment companies and those using broker loads. To achieve maximum distribution, many fund management companies registered the same portfolio, managed by the same investment professionals, in a variety of share classes. To combat the loss of the edge gained from selling proprietary products (which carried higher margins), the dominant fund distribution platforms adopted models predicated on "institutional due diligence" practices that promised to screen out all investment managers except "the very best."

The rationing of available space created opportunities to extract high account service rebates as a condition for placement on the platform. Increasing industry concentration among fund distributors and the registration of formerly no-load products in a variety of 12(b)-1 structures is illustrated in the accompanying figures. The name of the actual manager was removed from the exhibit because the practice is common, and hundreds, if not thousands, of investment managers might be used to illustrate the same point.

Table 1. *Actual Investment Returns from Same Investment Engine Marketed through Different Distribution Channels and 12(b)-1 Structures*[a]

| | Same fund large cap core | | | | |
	A	B	C	I	R
Morningstar ranking	3	3	3	4	4
Institutional class pricing	N	N	N	Y	N
Retirement class pricing	Y	Y	Y	N	Y
401K	Y	Y	Y	Y	Y
Load	Y	Y	Y	N	Y
Back end	C	C	C	N	N
Deferred fee	1	4	1	0	0
Front end fee	5.25	0	0	0	0
Expense ratio	1.14	1.91	1.91	0.89	1.39

Source: Based on data from eVestment Alliance.
a. The fund name was omitted because this example is easily extrapolated to thousands of management company products.

Adviser Profitability or Intermediary Profitability?

Table 1 illustrates five funds managed by the same fund management group, using the same strategy, each priced for different distribution channels. The effective expense ratio for B and C class shares is more than twice the expense ratio for investor-class shares. Pricing strategies have such an effect on investor results that the equivalent portfolio earns fewer stars in distribution channels in which advice carries a higher explicit cost. Table 2 displays annualized returns for the five mutual funds arrayed against peer group averages and quartile distributions for more than 1,000 large core mutual funds. Advice-class shares compound at an annualized rate that is 1.2 percent lower than the rate for investor-class shares, significantly reducing long-term returns. Figure 1 shows that the industry "cloning" of investment products for placement in different channels results in a substantially identical portfolio placing in different quartiles of long-term performance. Of the four funds offered to investors for at least five years, two earned returns above both the S&P 500 and the peer group median and two earned returns below both the S&P 500 and the peer group median. The difference reflected the impact of 12(b)-1 distribution fees. Figure 2 shows the true cost of advice over five years as investor-class shares cumulatively returned 10 percent more than B class shares. While hidden servicing costs and the asset size of each strategy complicate analysis, the profitability for each approach should be approximately sim-

Table 2. *Annual Return, Percent against 1,000 Plus Fund Peer Group*

		1 Year	3 Years	5 Years	10 Years
X	Large Cap Core B	14.10	14.74	15.38	NA
	Large Cap Core C	14.20	14.74	15.38	NA
	Large Cap Core I	15.36	15.92	16.58	NA
	Large Cap Core A	15.06	15.62	16.28	NA
	Large Cap Core R	14.77	15.30	NA	NA
S&P 500 Index		16.44	13.14	15.45	6.57
Universe (5 percent)		23.84	17.74	19.09	10.11
Universe (25 percent)		18.20	14.20	15.85	7.04
Universe (median)		16.12	12.86	14.77	6.21
Universe (75 percent)		14.26	11.73	13.39	5.16
Universe (95 percent)		9.82	9.21	11.11	3.29

Source: Based on eVestment Alliance.

ilar for the investment adviser. The strong and visible impact on long-term returns attributable to 12(b)-1 fees should make regulators take a deep breath as they consider questions related to assessment of such fees on index funds and closed strategies.[3]

Again, the BoardIQ roundtable suggests that "the selection of appropriate peer groups, like other aspects of the 15(c) review, may present certain gray areas. The panel recommends that trustees make sure the peer groups are not pieced together to make the fund look good."[4]

Can Anyone Define "Economies of Scale?"

Finally, trustees must look through a lens to determine *whether fees reflect economies of scale as the assets grow within a fund.* Again, BoardIQ reports that its panel of experts identified economies of scale as "one of the most difficult areas in the entire realm of 15(c) review . . . boards should keep asking the questions about economies of scale, but they caution trustees that economies of scale don't always apply . . . are not linear, nor easily measured."[5] Many defenders of industry pricing practices suggest that 12(b)-1 fees are essential for funds to achieve

3. The mutual fund industry appears to be conducting a hasty retreat from B class shares after recent breakpoint scandals and the accumulating evidence that advice must be superb to overcome the long-term performance drag.
4. BoardIQ, "Break the Boilerplate: Key Strategies for Evaluating Fund Advisory Fees," December 2007 (www.BoardIQ.com).
5. Ibid.

Figure 1. *Performance Measured against 1,000 Plus Mutual Fund Peer Group (U.S. Large Blend)*

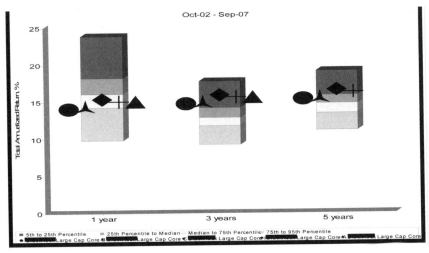

Source: Based on data from eVestment Alliance.

Figure 2. *Impact on Cumulative Returns over Time from 12(b)-1 Fees*

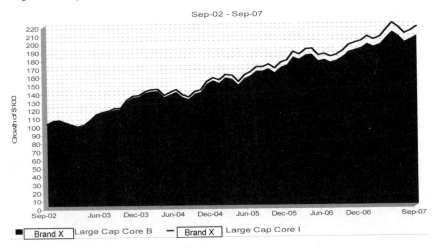

Source: Based on data from eVestment Alliance.

scale economics. One must ask whether a fund group like Capital Research, with more than $1 trillion of assets under management, has yet achieved scale. Further debasing this distribution-oriented argument is that all advisers, from the very largest to the newest entrant, pay exactly the same 12(b)-1 fees.

If, as suggested by the BoardIQ roundtable, industry experts cannot define or measure essential elements of mutual fund profitability on a fund-by-fund basis, understand comparability of pricing based on solid peer group metrics, or define what constitutes economies of scale in the mutual fund business, then I am flabbergasted at the industry costs associated with the annual 15(c) dance between boards and fund lawyers and executives. Investors are neither protected nor served. It is time to remove restrictions from price competition. After all, investors in mutual funds have virtually no switching costs if they use investor-class shares in today's NTF world.

Contributors

Harold Bradley
Kauffman Foundation

Yasuyuki Fuchita
*Nomura Institute of Capital Markets
Research*

Koichi Iwai
*Nomura Institute of Capital Markets
Research*

Ajay Khorana
Georgia Institute of Technology

Robert E. Litan
*Kauffman Foundation and Brookings
Institution*

Allan S. Mostoff
Mutual Fund Directors Forum

Brian Reid
Investment Company Institute

Henri Servaes
London Business School

Paula A. Tkac
Federal Reserve Bank of Atlanta

Peter Wallison
American Enterprise Institute

Index

Brookings Institution

The Brookings Institution is a private nonprofit organization devoted to research, education, and publication on important issues of domestic and foreign policy. Its principal purpose is to bring the highest quality independent research and analysis to bear on current and emerging policy problems. The Institution was founded on December 8, 1927, to merge the activities of the Institute for Government Research, founded in 1916, the Institute of Economics, founded in 1922, and the Robert Brookings Graduate School of Economics and Government, founded in 1924. Interpretations or conclusions in Brookings publications should be understood to be solely those of the authors.

Nomura Institute of Capital Markets Research

Established in April 2004 as a subsidiary of Nomura Holdings, Nomura Institute of Capital Markets Research (NICMR) offers original, neutral studies of Japanese and Western financial markets and policy proposals aimed at establishing a market-structured financial system in Japan and contributing to the healthy development of capital markets in China and other emerging markets. NICMR disseminates its research among Nomura Group companies and to a wider audience through regular publications in English and Japanese.

Tokyo Club Foundation for Global Studies

The Tokyo Club Foundation for Global Studies was established by Nomura Securities Co., Ltd., in 1987 as a nonprofit organization for promoting studies in the management of the global economy. It sponsors research, symposiums, and publications on global economic issues. The Tokyo Club has developed a network of institutions from Europe, the United States, and Asia that assists in organizing specific research programs and identifying appropriate expertise. In recent years, the research agenda has strongly focused on emerging trends in global capital markets as well as current issues in macro-economic stability and growth. Information about past and future programs may be viewed on the Foundation's website, www.tcf.or.jp/.

3987 118